SO-CAP-836

J'M BUTLER
11270 SHARRMONT CT.
GALT, CALIFORNIA 95632

LET GOD ARISE

Judson Cornwall, ThD.

OTHER BOOKS BY JUDSON CORNWALL

Let Us Praise
Let Us Draw Near
Let Us Abide
Let Us Enjoy Forgiveness
Let Us Be Holy
Heaven
Please Accept Me
Let Us See Jesus
Unfeigned Faith
Profiles of A Leader
Let Us Get Together
Let Us Worship
Elements of Worship
Incense and Insurrection ·
Meeting God
Worship As Jesus Taught It
Leaders, Eat What You Serve
The Secret of Personal Prayer
David Worshiped a Living God

1990 releases
Worship As David Lived It
Praying the Scriptures
The Five-Fold Foundation for Marriage

U.S.A. ADDRESS:
4335 E. Shangri-La
Phoenix, Arizona 85028

God is already arising!

Judson Cornwall

LET GOD ARISE

Psalm 68:1

Judson Cornwall, ThD.

Sharon Publications Limited
49 Coxtie Green Road
Pilgrims Hatch
Brentwood, Essex CM14 5PS

Unless otherwise identified, Scripture quotations are from the King James Version of the Bible.

Scripture quotations identified NIV are from HOLY BIBLE New International Version, copyright © 1971 by Tyndale House Publishers, Wheaton, IL. Used by permission.

Scripture quotations identified JERUSALEM are from The Jerusalem Bible, copyright © 1966 by Darton, Longman & Todd, Ltd., and Doubleday and Company, Inc. Used by permission of the publishers.

Scripture quotations identified PHILLIPS are from THE NEW TESTAMENT IN MODERN ENGLISH (Revised Edition), translated by J. B. Phillips. © J. B. Phillips 1958, 1960, 1972. Used by permission of Macmillan Publishing Co., Inc.

Scripture quotations identified RSV are from the Revised Standard Version of the Bible, copyrighted 1946, 1952, © 1971 and 1973.

Scripture quotations identified NEB are from *The New English Bible.* © The Delegates of the Oxford University Press and the Syndics of the Cambridge University Press 1961 and 1970. Reprinted by permission.

Scripture quotations identified MLB are from THE MODERN LANGUAGE BIBLE—THE NEW BERKELEY VERSION IN MODERN ENGLISH, Copyright 1945, 1959, © 1969 by Zondervan Publishing House, and are used by permission.

Scripture quotations identified AMPLIFIED are from AMPLIFIED BIBLE, OLD TESTAMENT, Copyright 1962, 1964 by Zondervan Publishing House and are used by permission.

Scripture quotations identified MOFFATT are from THE BIBLE: A NEW TRANSLATION by James Moffatt. Copyright 1954 by James A. R. Moffatt. By permission of Harper & Row, Publishers, Inc.

Scripture quotations identified ASV are from the American Standard Version of the Revised Bible, copyrighted 1946 by the International Council of Religious Education, and are used by permission.

Library of Congress Cataloging in Publication Data
Cornwall, Judson.
  Let God arise.
  1.Bible. O.T. Psalms LXVIII—Meditations.
  2.Bible. O.T. Psalms LXVIII—Commentaries.
BS1450 68th.C63   222'.2077   81-17951
ISBN 0-8007-5080-2   AACR2

Copyright © 1982 by Judson Cornwall
Published by Sharon Publications Limited
49 Coxtie Green Road, Pilgrims Hatch
Brentwood, Essex CM14 5PS
All rights reserved
Printed in England

TO the three churches I served in my thirty years of pastoring, from whom I probably learned more of God than I was able to teach:

Kennewick Assembly of Kennewick, Washington
Summitview Assembly of Yakima, Washington
Santa Clara Assembly of Eugene, Oregon

Contents

Preface

So much truth is lost by those who approach the Old Testament from a purely historical position. In writing about Israel's wanderings in the wilderness, Paul said, "Now all these things happened to them as examples, and they were written for our admonition, upon whom the ends of the ages have come" (1 Corinthians 10:11). This is more than ample authority for us to approach historic happenings in the Old Testment to make application to present day experience.

David was using this ploy in Psalm 68. His cry, "Let God arise," (Psalm 68:1) is a quote from the words of Moses. Every time the cloud of God's presence over the camp lifted and began to move, the ark of the covenant of the LORD was marched three days ahead of the rest of the camp while the priests sought a suitable campsite for such a large multitude of people. To alert the congregation of Israel that change was only three days away, Moses would cry out, "Rise up, O LORD! Let Your enemies be scattered, And let those who hate You flee before You" (Numbers 10:35).

David quoted: "Let God arise" as the cry of the watchmen in succeeding generations alerting the people of God to changes in God's relationship with them. We Christians of the twentieth-century need to realize that no matter how comfortable our camp may have become, God did not bring us out of our "Egypt" to live in a wilderness camp-site. He has purposed to bring us into "a land that flows with milk and honey." To lead us into His best God must direct us out of His good, and this has been a perpetual problem for the church which consistently enjoys sameness and resists change.

Perhaps we have forgotten that the ultimate purpose of all of God's leadership is to introduce Himself and His ways to us in a progressive revelation. No matter what we may know of God, there is far more to be learned. Every visitation of God has brought an increase of knowledge of the divine to His people, but it has also left a percentage of persons basking in the sunlight of past revelation. When will we learn that fresh revelation of God never violates or invalidates prior revelations? The new grows out of the old much as a tree grows out of its roots.

The goal of the church should reach beyond merely preserving the old. Every generation of Christians needs a fresh encounter with God that moves the church into a new encampment of God's provisions. Such a stirring is again coming to the Body of Christ. All over the earth men, women and children are hearing the cry, "Let God arise!", and they are packing their spiritual belongings, folding their tents, and preparing to follow the ark of the Lord into new territory. Just what this new territory will be like is not known. We do know that it will be God's provision for His chosen people, and it will have His presence and His protection. If we do not move on with God we had better be prepared to supply our own provisions and protection, or we will die in the wilderness remembering how good it used to be when God was in the midst of our camp.

The cry of the Spirit, "Let God arise!" will either induce excitement or exasperation. If we face the challenge of moving on in God we will be thrilled with the new knowledge about God that comes, but if we have become too comfortable and settled in our present encampment with God we may be disgusted at the prospect of change. Church history shows that one of these two extremes has always controlled the religious element in the day of divine visitation. We have no reason to expect it to be different in this hour when the trumpet is being blown and the prophets are crying, "Let God arise!"

David saw a continuing pattern of revelation of God in the encampment of Israel, and he progressively unfolds it before our eyes in this sixty-eighth Psalm. May God open our eyes to see that indeed, "The LORD is great and greatly to be praised" (1 Chronicles 16:25).

Judson Cornwall
Phoenix, Arizona
1989

LET GOD ARISE

1
God Arising

Let God arise, let his enemies be scattered; let them also that hate him flee before him. As smoke is driven away, so drive them away; as wax melteth before the fire, so let the wicked perish at the presence of God.

PSALMS 68:1–2

Never in their lifetime had these Israeli soldiers experienced such a beating as they had taken this day. On every front the Philistines had outmanned, outmanoeuvred, and outfought them. Hophni and Phinehas, sons of the aging, obese, and nearly blinded high priest Eli, could not demonstrate sufficient leadership to contain the Philistines and turn the tide of battle.

"Unless we do something dramatic right away we'll lose the war, and instead of having the Philistines enslaved, as we have had for the past decade, we will become their slaves," Phinehas declared.

"That will mean death for us and father Eli," Hophni sighed, "to say nothing of what they will do to our women, but at this point it almost seems inevitable."

"Don't give up so easily," Phinehas chided. "There must be something we can do to inspire these men of Israel to turn the tide of battle."

"Well, why don't we get the Ark of the Covenant and bring it into the battle?" suggested Hophni.

"Father would never consent to letting the Ark leave Shiloh," Phinehas retorted. "Besides, what makes you think that would change things?"

"During the conquest of this land the Ark always went into battle with Joshua, and he never lost a battle," Hophni said.

"I've heard that story a thousand times," replied Phinehas, "but I've always wondered if it was true."

"What have we to lose?" Hophni pointed out. "As things stand in this war we are as good as dead men anyway. Let's give the Ark a try. Father need never know about it."

Hastening back to Shiloh, they carried this visible symbol of the presence of Jehovah right into the encampment of Israel's fighting men, amidst the mixed reaction of holy awe on the part of some and excited shouting on the part of others.

Although the army was greatly impressed and inspired on the whole, apparently God was not, for He allowed the Ark to be captured in one of Israel's most ignominious defeats. The battle was lost; Hophni and Phinehas were killed; the Ark was captured, and when Eli was given the news he fell from his chair and broke his neck, thus ending forever the reign of the priesthood in Israel.

Confident that the Israelites would be their slaves forever, the Philistines carried the captured Ark of the Lord to Ashdod, where they placed it in the house of their chief deity, Dagon. Their celebration, however, was soon turned to consternation as Jehovah caused Dagon to fall and be broken and smote the populace with emerods. A council of the Philistine elders recommended the return of the Ark to Israel, so they sent it back on a new cart totally unattended. The Israelites were so excited to see the Ark returned that the men of Beth-shemesh looked into the Ark to see if the Philistines had removed any of its contents, and the wrath of God smote a tremendous number of them. Fearfully the Ark of God was sent to Kirjath-jearim for twenty years; it finally ended up in the house of Abinadab in Gibeah, and for two and a half generations the Ark was separated from the capital city of Israel.

Godly Samuel, the prophet-judge, never attempted to move it, nor did Saul, the first king of Israel. It was not until David had solidified Israel into a secure kingdom that a yearning for this visible symbol of God to be in Jerusalem caused David to build a cart, seeking to emulate the one-hundred-year-old action of the Philistines, and bring back the Ark. But this aborted attempt brought God's judgment on those who dared to touch the Ark.

After a search of the Scriptures to find the divinely appointed means of transporting the Ark, David once again initiated action to bring God's presence back to Jerusalem. Borne on the shoulders of specially consecrated priests, the Ark was carried six paces and then lowered to a resting place while sacrifices to God were made. The entire procession was one of song, dance, and mirth, for David was excited at the return of God's presence.

As an expression of that excitement, David composed this Sixty-eighth Psalm, which begins, "Let God arise . . ." God was returning to Jerusalem in a symbolic manner, and David cried, "Let God arise." It was to be a new day for Israel, for God had returned to them.

It is a new day for any people when God is invited to return as their sovereign Lord. The presence of the Lord is the difference between day and night or life and death in any religious body.

Tragically, just as Israel learned to function without the visible symbol of the presence of God, so most religious groups can adapt to the absence of God. But the absence of God is also an absence of love, light, fire, and holiness, for these are all a part of the essential nature of God. No matter what the theology is or what form of government may have been adopted, when God is in the midst of a people, it will be a loving people who have warmth, spiritual insight, and holy lives. Conversely, when God is left in the border cities and not brought into the centre of activity, there is a cold, calloused, legalistic relationship that tends to a rigid conformity rather than a real confrontation with God which would infuse the divine nature into the participants.

If David ever wrote a verse that needs to become the survival cry of today's church, it is "Let God arise." We need the presence of God in a fresh new way. We need the counsel of God, which was always communicated from between the faces of the Cherubim on the Mercy Seat that formed the lid of the Ark of the Covenant. We need the guidance that the Ark had given to Israel, and we desperately need the protection that God's presence always affords. Return, O Lord, unto Thy people. "Let God arise." Bring Thy presence back to Thy people, O God. Doctrine we know; structure we know; but unless we have Thy presence we cannot know Thee.

Although this is indeed a psalm of David, the initial cry is probably a quote from Moses, for during the wilderness wanderings, every time the cloud lifted to lead the encampment to another site, Moses cried, "Rise up, Lord, and let thine enemies be scattered; and let them that hate thee flee before thee" (Numbers 10:35). It was the cry of change. It was the call to progress. This cry of Moses caused the entire camp to prepare to move on with God.

Immediately, the Levites who were charged with the carrying of the Ark went into the Holy of Holies, took down the separating veil and used it as a cover for the Ark, and then put their shoulders to the staves and followed the moving cloud. The rest of the priests attended to the dismantling of the Tabernacle and subsequently followed the Ark. The camp of Israel had three days to fold their tents and follow the wagons carrying the Tabernacle. There was no place for argument and no time for delay. God was moving and His people must move with Him! Not once did Moses initiate a move; it was always God leading His people onward.

It would violate our understanding of human nature to suppose that everyone in Israel was pleased and anxious to move to another campsite, for most of us prefer constancy to change. We love the security of sameness, and it is very likely that they did too.

It does not take an unusually vivid imagination to picture a scene like this: Abie ran into his tent with the great news. "Sari, the watchmen have just come to our tribe to inform us that God is arising. We'll have to start packing immediately."

"Oh, no, you don't," Sari replied. "I've had just about enough of your moving the family every two or three months. Mother told me I would come to no good if I married you. I've had to move nine times since we fled Egypt, and I'm just not going to move again."

"But, Sari," Abie reasoned, "God is moving the entire camp. We don't dare stay here by ourselves; besides, what would the others think of us if we didn't move with God?"

"I don't care what they think," Sari yelled. "I only wish you cared what I thought for a change. We're comfortably settled here, and I have no intention of moving one foot away from here."

Unable to move his wife, Abie stayed with her as they bade farewell to their relatives and friends. But as the great multitude of people marched out across the wastelands, Abie and Sari began to feel the heat of the desert sun in a far more intense manner than ever before, for the sheltering cloud that had always covered the camp was now advancing with the camp. Worse than that, the pillar of fire also departed with the camp, leaving the family shivering in the desert night. Their's was a troubled sleep that night, for they had never experienced such silence in all of their lives.

"Never you mind," Sari said in the morning. "I'll make your favorite breakfast as soon as I return from gathering manna."

But, of course, there was no manna to be gathered, for the manna came down under the perimeter of the cloud, and the cloud had departed.

As they met back at the tent, Sari showed her empty manna bucket, only to observe Abie's equally empty water skin. "The rock that supplies the water moved with the camp," he explained.

When they realized that all of God's provisions and protection were available only in His presence, it didn't take Abie and Sari very long to pack their belongings and hastily march in the direction they had seen the rest of the encampment take, for without God, life was impossible in their barren wasteland.

It will always be so. No matter how beautiful the trappings are, or how learned the practitioners of religion may be, without the presence of God there is nothing that meets the needs of man's spirit. Only the waters of the Holy Spirit can quench man's thirst, and only the Bread of Heaven can satisfy his hunger. God's provision for man's needs is always tied to God's presence. Where He abides there's all else besides. God's presence is the key to God's presents.

Israel wandered in the wilderness for forty years but never lacked any provision as long as they had God's presence. God led, fed, guided, and guarded them twenty-four hours of the day. Nevertheless, all of this was contingent upon their remaining with God.

Historically we Christians have proved our unwillingness to continue to progress with God. We accept His divine leadership out of sin and the kingdom of satan and often move with Him into the provision of water and manna, but soon we tire of the nomadic way of life and want something more permanent. Every major move of God that brought revival or renewal has led people from one encampment of discovery to a new revelation of God, His ways, or His provisions. Those who dared to move with God into new truth were usually persecuted by those who refused to budge from "the old ways," and soon these oppressed ones who banded together for mutual protection and fellowship inadvertently formed an organization which grew into a denomination. Their immediate goals of codifying the revealed truth and teaching it to others necessitated the formation of publishing houses and Bible schools, and the eager graduates fanned throughout the nation pioneering new churches to propagate these fresh truths. By the time the fledgling organization gained acceptance in the major religious bodies, the trumpet sounded, and someone cried, "Let God arise!"

"Oh, no," the leaders protested. "We've just dedicated our national headquarters. We can't walk off and leave all of this."

Generally it is only a small group of the spiritually hungry and those discontent with the status quo who walk from this great encampment into the unknown with God, where fresh revelation is given and life flows abundantly. They, too, are persecuted by the group that a few decades before had been the persecuted, so they band together for protection and comfort, and before long they, too, are building their permanent dwelling place in God's provision.

Will we ever learn that ". . . here have we no continuing city, but we seek one to come" (Hebrews 11:13), we need to constantly remind ourselves that we have not yet arrived. This camping place may be superior to the preceding one, but it is not yet God's ultimate for the believer. Only a conquered Promised Land will fulfill our inheritance. Until then, we are progressing from faith to faith and from grace to grace.

When God arises and begins to lead into new territory, those who move with Him bring everything they have gained up to this point in their journey and enjoy the continued provision, protection, and presence of God. There should be no insecurity, for they have abandoned nothing but an old campsite that was becoming hopelessly defiled anyway. Only if their security was in a specific location (or doctine, or practice, and so forth) should they feel uncomfortable in moving on with God. Nothing else changes.

David (as well as Moses) recognized that when God arose, His people were going to be led into something even greater, but the enemies of God would be threatened hopelessly. "Let God arise, let his enemies be scattered," the psalmist wrote. Like the demon in Gaderea who met Christ with the cry "What have I to do with thee, Jesus, thou Son of the most high God? I adjure thee by God, that thou torment me not" (Mark 5:7), the enemies of God are never happy to have Him in their territory. Every move of God means a movement in the enemy camp, for the presence of God is threatening to all who oppose and hate Him.

Three classes of enemies are listed by David, and he skillfully uses three separate Hebrew words to delineate them. In crying, "Let God arise, let his *enemies* be scattered," David used the Hebrew word *oyeb*, which fundamentally means "adversary." When Peter challenged the Christians to "be sober, be vigilant," it was "because your *adversary* the devil, as a roaring lion, walketh about, seeking whom he may devour" (1 Peter 5:8, italics added). Hence "adversary" is a title applied to satan, and it is a fitting appellation since the devil is an adversary both to God and man. He sought to overthrow God in heaven, and failing in that, he has sought to overthrow man on earth. No work in the Kingdom of God ever progresses without a challenge by the adversary, and none have met the Christ of the cross without subsequently meeting this satanic adversary who challenged, "Hath God said?" (Genesis 3:1).

In some Christian circles it is popular to deny the existence of this adversary, but Peter, awaiting his execution in prison, and Paul and Silas, in the Philippian dungeon, knew only too well what a forceful person this adversary really is. Denial of his existence does not hinder his activity. He loves to work unobtrusively, allowing others to get the credit for his opposition.

In still other Christian circles the presence and power of this great adversary of the Church is greatly overempha sized. He is regularly rebuked, cast out, and contested with. Sometimes he is given more attention than the Lord Jesus Christ, and these Christians spend more time resisting satan than they spend responding to the Lord.

David strikes a proper balance. "Let God arise, let his enemies be scattered," (Psalms 68:1) he says. When God arises, this great adversary is scattered very much as smoke is driven away by a strong breeze. God is still our best defense against the satanic. Satan's kingdom is a kingdom of darkness (*see* Ephesians 6:12), while ". . . God is light, and in him is no darkness at all" (1 John 1:5). What happens to darkness when light comes in? It flees, or is dispelled at the speed of 186,000 miles per second (the speed of light) and in ratio to the intensity of the light. The greater the density of light, the greater is the dispersion of the darkness. The answer to darkness is not to fight it but to light it, since darkness is fundementally the absence of light. Similarly, the answer to the adversary is not so much to engage him in confrontation as to expose him to the presence of God. When God is lifted up in our lives, the adversary is expelled by the very light of that divine presence. God in the midst of His Church is still the best answer to satanic infiltration. "Let God arise, let his *adversary* be scattered."

David's second class of enemies is called "them also that hate him" for which he uses the Hebrew word *sane* for the haters. This word literally means "to hate personally, or to be hateful or utterly odious." We commonly think of those who hate God as being outside the ranks of the Church and probably deeply involved in works of iniquity, but church history does not confirm this. The most serious inquisitions, persecutions, and religious oppressions have come from within the Church, not from without.

Perhaps this would be less confusing if we would remind ourselves that the original sin was not merely a sin of pride but a sin of exercising a will against the will of God. For all time there had been none but the divine will of God until

Lucifer began saying, "I will . . . I will . . ." (*see* Isaiah 14:12–14). Five times Lucifer exerted his will against the will of God, forcing his own expulsion from heaven; but his demotion did not cancel his expressed will, so for the first time in the history of God there were two wills. The angelic force divided itself between these two wills, and many of the angels followed Lucifer out of heaven.

When God created man He gave him a free will. The early days of the garden existence saw man's will perfectly united with the will of God, but satan reasoned that if he could get man to submit his will to him, there might still be a chance for the will of Lucifer to prevail over the will of God, especially in the light of man's power of procreation. The temptation of man was supposed to cause man to surrender his will to satan, but it ended merely in the introduction of a third will into the universe as Adam's action said, "I will." The conflict though the ages has been to cause man to surrender his will. Satan has used force, coercion, fear, threats, and blackmail. He has bribed, promised, bragged, and begged, but his successes are usually very short-lived. No matter how high satan may elevate a man, or how much of this world's power and goods he may share with him, there consistently seems to come the time when that man exercises his own will, thereby violating his contract with satan.

In contrast to this, "God commendeth his love towards us, in that, while we were yet sinners, Christ died for us" (Romans 5:8), and men, women, boys, and girls surrender their lives to Christ in such consecration as to thrust them onto the mission fields, place them in ministry, cause them to give liberally of their finances, or face the death of martyrdom cheerfully. "Our wills are ours to make them Thine," is the cry of their lives.

Christ came to bring us back into the singular will of God, but the Church is still filled with people who want their own way. Oftentimes they desire to have great authority and power over the lives of other Christians and to establish the policy that will determine how these people worship God. Frequently these strong-willed individuals fight for governmental positions in the churches and vie for the highest titles available. They want neither God nor His will; they want their way, their work, and their will. They are haters of God's will and therefore are haters of God. Jesus Christ Himself would not be allowed to join some of the churches in America even if He signed a membership application.

From time to time churches have sought to purge such individuals from their memberships in an attempt to purify the body, but the answer to the presence of self-willed individuals in the leadership of the church is not church discipline so much as the divine presence. When God arises, those that hate Him flee from Him, for when God's will is exercised, all human will is superseded. Where God is King, all others are subservient to Him. Where God's authority is embraced, all other authority is emaciated. The vital, living presence of God is still the best answer to the violent lusting for power that tears at the very soul of many of our church organizations. "Let God arise, . . . let them also that hate him flee before him" (Psalms 68:1).

In addition to scattering the adversary and causing the haters of God to flee before Him as smoke in a wind, David says that ". . . the *wicked* [Hebrew: *rasha'*] perish at the presence of God" (Psalms 68:2, italics added). In his book *Synonyms of the Old Testament*, Robert Baker Girdlestone says that *rasha'* speaks of "the *activity*, the *tossing*, and the *confusion* in which the wicked live, and the perpetual agitation which they cause to others." The word *wicked* in this verse is as concerned with wickedness as with the wicked person.

Just as one of the fundamental characteristics of the Christian is righteousness and peace, the outstanding characteristic of the wicked individual is the perpetual agitation which he causes in others. If the alcoholic affected only himself, society would not have such a problem with drinking, but the wife and children, the employer, and the friends and acquaintances of the problem drinker are all critically affected by his moral wrongness. He creates a tossing and confusion that engulf others like a vortex.

So does all moral wrongness. The abuser of drugs may declare that it is his body that he is hurting and it is none of our business what he does to it, but it is our goods he steals to support his habit, and it is our taxes that provide hospitalization or prison care for him. His way of life fosters fear in society. It is an agitation to all.

Christians are vitally affected by moral wrongness. The tension that sin produces affects our emotions; the cost of sin increases our taxes; the filth of sin pollutes our minds, and the disintegration of society affects our homes. The activity, the tossing, and the confusion in which the wicked live, and the perpetual agitation which they cause others, as Girdlestone puts it, leave their mark on Christian individuals, Christian homes, and Christian churches. The wicked man does not live unto himself; he affects all of us, for wickedness does not merely affect the damned but affects the righteous as well. We could well wish for a total Christian society where no unrighteousness could exist, but that utopia will not be our inheritance until after Jesus comes. Heaven will be such a place, but this is not yet heaven!

Comfortingly, David declared that ". . . as wax melteth before the fire, so let the wicked (*rasha'*) perish at the presence of God" (Psalms 68:2). The fire of God's presence melts the effects of wickedness just as the flame melts the candle wax. Nothing can clean the mind of a Christian believer faster than a little time spent in the presence of God. Even a home that has been disturbed by unrighteous behaviour can come to peace when there is a recognition of the presence of the Lord. Churches undergoing pressure from wickedness in their communities can find renewed peace, hope, and love when God is allowed to arise in their midst. "Let God arise . . . so let the wicked perish at the presence of God" (Psalms 68:1,2).

To the English reader the wording "Let God arise" seems to call for permission ro arise, but nothing could be further from the truth or from the construction of the Hebrew. None need give God permission to arise; He is God and will do whatever pleases Him. Moses never called to God to arise; he called to the people to inform them that God was rising. The Berkeley translation of the Bible puts this verse in a future tense in saying, "God shall arise . . .," and our hearts say amen! The thrust of the entire Bible is that God in His sovereignty will reign in both His church and His world. Adversaries, haters, and the wicked will be totally removed from God's Kingdom, and we who love His appearing will enjoy His presence without mixture, without interference, and without opposition. God shall, indeed, arise.

The translators of the Amplified Bible offer an even more exciting concept of this verse in saying, "God is [already] beginning to arise." We need not grant Him permission to arise, and we need not await some future date of His arising, for God is already beginning to arise. The portents of His presence are among us already. God's presence is available to us now through the offices of the Holy Spirit. God's presence is available to any church which invites Him and makes room for Him in their midst. God's light is now shining, dispelling the darkness, and those who choose to do so can "walk in the light, as he is in the light" (1 John 1:7).

God in our midst means peace instead of strife, provision instead of poverty, love instead of hate, and an advocate instead of an adversary; but even more than this, God's presence among His people brings revelation as to His person. We come to know God by fellowshipping with God. It is out of relationship that revelation of God flows, so when God arises, the knowledge of God increases. Until His presence is recognized, welcomed, and embraced, we will never really know God, for instance, "Our Father which art in heaven . . ." (Matthew 6:9).

2
God Fathering

A father of the fatherless, and a judge of the widows, is God in his holy habitation. God setteth the solitary in families: he bringeth out those which are bound with chains: but the rebellious dwell in a dry land.

PSALMS 68:5–6

In a psalm that so vividly depicts God in action with His people, it seems fitting that following His arising, the first word picture David paints is that of God fathering. "A father of the fatherless," verse five begins, and then it lists four classes of people over whom God exercises a fatherly responsibility: the orphans, the widows, the solitary, and the prisoners.

"Father" is a consistent Bible title for God. Jesus Himself used it over 175 times in the Gospels, and the New Testament writers used it an additional 78 times in the remaining New Testament books. The expression "God our Father" was such a Pauline favorite that he used it in every book of the New Testament he wrote. When the disciples asked for a model prayer, Jesus taught them to address their prayers to "Our Father which art in heaven" (Matthew 6:9). Furthermore, Jesus referred to God as "My Father" (Matthew 16:17), "our Father" (Luke 11:2), "your Father" (John 20:17), and "Abba, Father" (Mark 14:36). The fatherhood of God is indisputable. It is probably the first concept of God that is taught to us following our conversion.

God Fathering the Fatherless – Security

Although the Bible consistently reveals God as the Father of mankind, the fifth and sixth verses of Psalm Sixty-eight speak of Him as Father to those over whom He would not normally have any responsibility. They are now viewed as His progeny, but by grace extended they are vaulted under the protectorate of God, who extends the same fathering care that a good earthly father would.

In a very *literal* sense God shows parental concern over the fatherless, the orphans, for by nature God is tender, merciful, and good, and this is consistently extended to the helpless and the sorrowful. The Old Testament law made provision for the care and protection of the orphans and the fatherless. Even their inheritance rights were protected by law. The New Testament, also, makes provision for Christian concern for the orphans, for James wrote, "Pure religion and undefiled before God and the Father is this, To visit the fatherless and widows in their affliction . . ." (James 1:27).

Since God classifies Himself as a Father of the fatherless, the church which represents the body of God's Son here on earth should also extend a practical concern to the fatherless, and our high divorce rate has given us many fatherless children in all of the churches. Doesn't God hear the cry of their loneliness in the twentiety century as well as He did in David's day?

In a strictly *social* sense God is equally a Father to the fatherless. Those who have been deserted by their friends, or who have been called (or forced) to leave father and mother for the sake of Christ and His Gospel, seem to find a special place in the heart of God, for Jesus assured us that "every one that hath forsaken houses, or brethren, or sisters, or father, or mother, or wife, or children, or lands, for my name's sake, shall receive an hundredfold, and shall inherit everlasting life" (Matthew 19:29). There is a special parental care that God exercises over those who lose their family relationship because of the Gospel, and God pledges that He will be their source of protection, provision, comfort, and instruction.

While this may have little meaning to those of us in the American culture who rarely face ostracism because of our religious beliefs (those of the Orthodox Jewish faith being a notable exception), other cultures, such as India, have such a tight family caste that the religious beliefs are predetermined for the children, and any violation of these beliefs becomes grounds for expulsion from the family. The hardships this imposes on Christian converts have been well-chronicled for us by missionaries to India and various Oriental lands. But where acceptance of Christ means the loss of a family, God declares Himself to be available as Father to them. "When my father and my mother forsake me, then the Lord will take me up," David cried (Psalms 27:10). God is, indeed, "a father of the fatherless."

Even in a *spiritual* sense God is a Father of the fatherless. The book of beginnings, Genesis, teaches us that man was made in the image of God as a son of God, and the intimate relationship between God and man is pictured as a walking and talking together in Eden's garden. But through the temptation of satan, man left God and embraced a pseudofather, very much as thousands of teenage children have fled American homes as runaways and have reached out to idealogies, religious cults, and strangers for the relationship that should have been provided by their earthly fathers.

Similarly, mankind in general has forsaken a family relationship with God and has embraced a relationship with this world system to the point where Jesus declared, "Ye are of your father, the devil . . ." (John 8:44). Jesus was not declaring that the devil had brought them into being, for he lacks creative power, but that there had been a turning from the Creator to the usurper-prince of this world as an embracing of a substitute for the Fatherhood of God. Like the prodigal son, those who leave Father's home are soon abandoned, forsaken, rejected, and ruined, and what seemed like the right way had as its end the ways of death.

The prophet Hosea, who ministered to a generation who had departed from God, ends his book in confessing to God, ". . . neither will we say any more to the work of our hands, Ye are our gods: for in thee the fatherless findeth mercy" (Hosea 14:3). While we Americans may not carve or cast idols, as some people have done, we do tend to worship science, the mind, the body, pleasure, and so forth. There are many things under our control to which our response is akin to biblical worship, and we tend to look to these for our guidance, comfort, and security. How carefully we Christians must walk the line between loving this country God has been kind enough to let us live in, and worshiping it. Socialism and humanism have so crept into our way of life as to cause us to believe that Washington D.C., is our God, our "great father" who will protect, provide, guide, and comfort us in our old age. But Uncle Sam is nothing more than the "work of our hands" which Hosea declared must be abandoned in order for us to reaffirm that ". . . in thee the fatherless findeth mercy."

The prodigal found mercy in the heart of the father when he returned, and so has every other fugitive son of the Father; no returning runaway has ever been rejected, or ever will be. The problem is not the forgiveness and acceptance of the Father, for that has been vouchsafed by promise, but the intricacy of the return is learning to accept ourselves so that we can walk as His children in love. He is the Father to the runaways.

I might suggest that this passage may have a more *intimate* sense of God's being a Father of the fatherless, for I remember that when Jesus told His disciples of His impending departure, He assured them, "I will not leave you comfortless: I will come to you" (John 14:18). The Living

Bible translates it, "No, I will not abandon you or leave you as orphans in the storm – I will come to you." The New International Version and the Jerusalem Bible also use the word *orphans* instead of the King James word *comfortless*. The promised Holy Spirit offers the intimacy of the Father on an everyday basis, for God is Father not merely in name; He is Father in nature, manifestation, provision, and fellowship as well. God enjoys fellowship with us; He chooses to be interested in those things that interest us, and He seeks to interest us in the things of His realm.

Those who walk with God need never be insecure, for God, the Father, is their security. A few years ago a small plane crash-landed in the backcountry of Alaska. The pilot and a teenage boy survived the crash with only minor injuries, and after waiting two days to be rescued, set out on foot to find help. After walking across the frozen and snow-covered tundra for over a week, they were rescued and rushed by air to a hospital for treatment. Asked by the reporters if he hadn't been terrified during his ordeal, the teenager replied, "No, you see, I was walking out with my father."

It is not where we are, but who we are that determines our security!

God Fathering the Widows – Equity

God is not only a Father to the fatherless; He is called "a judge of the widows" (Psalms 68:5). The Hebrew word translated "judge" in the King James Bible is *dayan* and is translated this way only twice in the entire Old Testament. It more literally means "advocate," and other translators use the word "champion" (Modern Language), "protector" (Revised Standard Version), and "defender" (Jerusalem Bible). That God is an advocate, protector, champion, and defender of widows is consistently confirmed in the Word.

The law provided, "Ye shall not afflict any widow, or fatherless child. If thou afflict them in any wise, and they cry at all unto me, I will surely hear their cry; And my wrath shall wax hot, and I will kill you with the sword . . ." (Exodus 22:22–24); and at the reaffirmation of the law to the second generation it was recorded, "For the Lord your God is God of gods, and Lord of lords, a great God . . . He doth execute the judgment of the fatherless and widow, and loveth the stranger, in giving him food and raiment" (Deuteronomy 10:17,18).

If the concept of fathering the fatherless speaks of security, then the characterization of God extending His robes of authority to be a Judge of the widows would speak of equity. In non-Christian cultures from antiquity until the present day the lot of the widow has been a vulnerable one, often without sound legal recourse, but wherever the Bible has become the basis for the laws of a land, there has been protection of a widow's rights and provision for her needs. Many a Christian widow has found such an advocate in God that she has referred to Him as her "husband," but however comforting that thought might be to her, this passage does not affirm that God is faithfully acting as an Advocate for His wife, for we would expect God to love His Bride, the Church. This passage does not say that as Father He is deeply in love with His wife, but it says that as Father He is sufficiently secure to reach beyond His commitments and offer Himself as a defender of the widows.

Would there not also be a *spiritual* sense in which God is said to be "a judge of the widows"? From the God-ward side we might say that the whole Church of Christ is now in a widowhood estate. Christ, her Bridegroom, died and ascended into heaven. Although His return is assured, the Church lives in a state of separation from her husband, anticipating His return when He will come and take her to Himself, and she will remember the reproach of her widowhood no longer. During this interim, however, God is the Church's Judge, Protector, Defender, Champion, and Advocate. The rights of the Church are safeguarded by the intervention of our Heavenly Father who is "a judge of the widows."

Even from the manward side we might say that individuals who entered into a bride relationship with God may through neglect or rebellion lose this intimate relationship with God. They may consider themselves divorced from God, but God never accepts their departure as a divorce. He told Israel, through the prophets, "Turn, O backsliding children, saith the Lord; for I am married unto you . . ." (Jeremiah 3:14). Even when the widowhood is of our choosing (divorce), God remains our Advocate. "And if any man sin, we have an advocate with the Father, Jesus Christ the righteous" (1 John 2:1). We may wander from Him looking for other lovers only to discover the emptiness and disappointment that all departure from God brings, but how can we come back to God after having so completely violated a pure relationship? Praise the Lord, we have an Advocate with the Father. There is a Helper, there is a Champion, a Defender, one who will plead our cause.

God is a Judge of the widows, and He never signs the divorce decree. He will bring together that which has been separated through pride and sin. By His action our rights are secured; our relationship awaits restoration, and our widowhood can be replaced with renewed commitment to marriage, because God has chosen to be the Advocate of the widow.

God Fathering the Solitary – Unity

The third class of people over which God exercises a fatherhood is the solitary: "God setteth the solitary in families . . ." or, as the Jerusalem Bible translates it, "God gives the lonely a permanent home" (Psalms 68:6). If the first group, the orphans, come into *security* as God fathers them, and the second class, the widows, come into *equity* under the fathering of God, then we could say that the solitary come into *unity* when God begins to father them.

In a very *literal* way God sets the solitary in families. The Jewish writers consistently understand this to mean an increase of families, with children in lawful marriage, and they love to illustrate it with Abraham and Sarah of the Bible. The Jewish *Targum* paraphrases these words to say, "God is He that joins couples, single ones into a couple, as one"; and some copies add "to build a house out of them."

God does bring individuals together and place them in couples to form a home so that out of the solitary can come a setting together in families. We've had a period here in America when it has been very popular to make light of marriage and try to find an alternate life-style. While the period is not over, it has crested and is on the decline. This generation has discovered what preceding generations discovered long ago – that without the family there is no security, no continuity, and no progeny.

At the root of all human society lies the institution of the family, and in the family we have a miniature picture of society. The home is both the first church and the first state. History will show us that every attempt to drastically alter society has required a drastic alteration in the family. One of the first actions of any dictator is to snatch the children from the home and put them in government-sponsored day-care centres so they can be indoctrinated with the new political philosophy at a tender age. Out of this comes a severe alteration in the family, and from this altered family comes an alteration in the state. Amazingly, it doesn't take long to accomplish this. How Christians need to guard the sanctity of the home in these days of increased emphasis on humanism, which tends to destroy the leadership of the home in teaching the rights of the individuals of the home!

To accept the Bible as our guide is to believe that the family is divine in its origin. It was instituted in Eden by God Himself for the preservation of the race and for the happiness of His creatures, and though sin may have corrupted it, satan has not destroyed the home, for Christ came to Calvary to reestablish the Christian home.

The family has well been defined as "the institute of the affections." It is the home of love – the place where the affectionate side of human nature receives its strongest impulse, its freest and fullest development. We're made for this, and we cannot function well without it. We can substitute for it, but we will never be complete without it. No nation has survived long after the family unit has disintegrated, and unless there comes a healing in the families of America, there is not going to be a healing in our nation. But "God setteth the solitary in families."

Beyond the literal sense there is also a *social* sense in which "God setteth the solitary in families." Probably most of us know what it is like to feel solitary, to be lonely, without companions, and with no one to sympathize with us or to understand us. It is the heaviest weight of being a stranger, whether through moving to a new community, changing schools, or merely being in another city on business or recreation. Even visiting a different church can be a lonely experience.

Fortunately, God has so united His children into one great family that no matter where they go they need not be solitary and desolate. Christians respond to Christians in spite of doctrinal differences, for it is a common life, not common beliefs, that unites them. The Christian brotherhood transcends cultural and language barriers. I have ministered in twenty-two countries of the world, few of them English speaking. My anticipated loneliness did not materialize when I realized that we were brothers in God – blood brothers in Christ – united by a common life. While communication was difficult, love flowed without hesitation.

I found fellowship in the Word, although we were reading it in different languages, and learned that a hug means the same thing in any language.

We may not have met before, but we Christians have the same Father and the same Elder Brother. We do not need to go to a bar to find companionship, for we have such a large family that members live in every country of the world. Some years ago I was coerced into ministering in a Catholic monastery in Northern California. As a staunch Protestant I had long ago classified the Catholics as "the enemy," so I dreaded the assignment and feared for my life for the first few minutes of my time in the abbey. However, I was so warmly received by the abbot and was given such gracious liberty to speak to the brothers about the Holy Spirit, and later asked to lay hands on them and pray for them, that I relaxed and began to realize that the entire family of god does not belong to my denomination. When the service was over, about two hours later, the abbot invited me to sing a song with the men of the abbey.

"I'm afraid I don't know any Catholic songs," I said.

"Oh, I think you'll know this one," the abbot assured me, and then he called a number, gave a musical pitch, and the brothers began to sing. "The Church's one foundation is Jesus Christ Her Lord. . . ." When the shock of hearing them sing a "Protestant" hymn wore off, I stood and joined them in as strong a bass voice as I could muster.

In a most marvelous manner, "God setteth the solitary in families." We love with the same love, we live by the same life, and we sing the same songs of praise and adoration to our common Father. What a family! As is often sung in our generation:

I'm so glad I'm part of the family of God;
I'm washed in the fountain, cleansed by His blood.
Joint heir with Jesus as I travel this sod;
I'm a part of the family, the family of God.

Who but God could bring a sinner who has lived a solitary life without God into fellowship with Himself and His Church? Those who were alienated from the life of God through ignorance are drawn through Christ. Although they once dwelt in their sensual self, not having the Spirit, and destitute of faith, hope, and love, they now become part of the family of God.

This Church of Jesus Christ, which is also called the family of God, has saints of various ages, sizes, and standing; some fathers, some young men, and some children. There is an age and experience level for everyone. Family government over all of them is provided in the church, and faithful stewards of the Word direct and regulate this great family of God. God has not merely redeemed many individuals; He has formed them into a family. He has brought unity without having to produce uniformity. Although there is a difference, there is also discipline. There is variety, but there is harmony, because it is "God [who] setteth the solitary in families." The Church is not always excited over whom God sets in the family, for it seems that He often chooses the wrong persons, but children come into the home not through a democratic vote, but as the direct result of a love relationship between the father and the mother. As the early church found out, "And the Lord added to the church daily such as should be saved" (Acts 2:47).

God Fathering the Prisoners – Liberty

The fourth group over which God exercises a fatherly care is the prisoners: "He bringeth out those which are bound with chains," or, as the Jerusalem Bible puts it, He "makes prisoners happy by setting them free . . ." (Psalms 68:6).

Literally God is for the release of the prisoner, especially those who are imprisoned for political or religious purposes. Peter found this out when the angel awakened him to release him from the prison in Jerusalem, and Paul and Silas rejoiced in the revelation of this truth when God sent an earthquake to release them from the dungeon in Philippi. Here in America we receive reports of thousands of prisoners who have found Jesus Christ as their Saviour and are enjoying a freedom in Him in spite of the prison walls.

However true this may be, the *spiritual* sense in which God "bringeth out those which are bound with chains" is far greater. The *Septuagint* and *Vulgate* Latin versions render this verse, "He bringeth forth the prisoners with fortitude." The thrust of the Hebrew seems to be that with a mighty hand God releases His children from habits, attitudes, inhibitions, and religious restrictions that have become personal prison cells, seriously restricting their liberty in Christ and His Church.

Many Christians are bound by the words of other people, while others are prisoners of fear or of failure. Some are restricted from enjoying an abundant life in Christ by memories of their unregenerate lives that seem to constantly underscore their unworthiness, while still others are so restricted by a poverty syndrome that they cannot accept and enjoy God's liberality to them.

God purposes to bring out those who are bound in order for them to learn to enjoy living a life in warm relationship with God. Moffatt translates this verse, ". . . and frees the prisoner for prosperity," while A. R. Fausset, in his *Critical Commentary on the Old Testament*, translates it, "He bringeth out those which are bound to prosperities – to all kinds of prosperity." God does not merely deliver from – He also delivers unto. The chains of sin have been broken by the power of Christ's cross, and the former servant of sin becomes a son of God. Those who had been led captive by satan have been proclaimed free by Father God and are now led by the Spirit. Prisoners of fear have been brought into faith, and prisoners of hope have been brought into realization of those hopes. Slaves of superstition have become students of the Scriptures, and men impoverished by the high cost of sinning have found their wages more than sufficient for comfortable living when love, joy, and peace are not purchased by the pint.

God wants us to be free from the success of satan's subtle attacks upon us. He has declared, "Ye shall know the truth, and the truth shall make you free. . . . If the Son therefore shall make you free, ye shall be free indeed" (John 8:32,36).

"Let God arise . . ." for as a Father of the fatherless it will bring us *security*. As "judge of the widow" it will bring us *equity*. As the Father placing "the solitary in families" it will bring us *unity*, and when Father releases us from captivity it brings us into *liberty*. These four things for which Americans strive ceaselessly are by-products of an intimate relationship with a Heavenly Father.

Furthermore, we do not need to fear our inability to enter into such a Fatherhood as God is offering us, for He is not *sending* us into security, equity, unity, and liberty; He is *taking us there. God leads* His people into new victories; but that's another story.

3
God Leading

O God, when thou wentest forth before thy people, when thou didst march through the wilderness; Selah: The earth shook, the heavens also dropped at the presence of God: even Sinai itself was moved at the presence of God, the God of Israel. Thou O God, didst send a plentiful rain, whereby thou didst confirm thine inheritance, when it was weary. The congregation hath dwelt therein: thou O God, hast prepared of thy goodness for the poor.

PSALMS 68:7–10

When the cry "Let God arise" echoes through the Church of the living God, it signifies that God is about to lead His people into new territory from victory to victory. God is never a follower; He is always a leader, and no matter what imagery the Scriptures may use, He is always pictured as a superior leader. Moses leading the people into the Promised Land are but weak characterizations of God's leadership, for God leads from a position of inherent strength and does not draw support from His followers, whereas Moses needed the strength of the seventy elders. God leads from a position of experience, for He, and He alone, has been this way before, but Moses admitted that he was in unfamiliar territory. Furthermore, God leads from a position of inherent authority; Moses and Joshua had only conferred authority. There is no higher authority known to mankind than God's authority.

Unquestionably, then, God is the perfect leader, and we desperately need His leadership, for as surely as Israel did not know her way through the desert, we do not know our way through life. Even after being brought out of sin, we do not know how to walk in righteousness. But, fortunately, we do not need to know, for God will lead us every step of the way. Psalms 68:7–9 illustrates at least six aspects of God's leadership.

God Goes Before

David cried, "O God, when thou wentest forth before thy people . . ." (Psalms 68:7), to which the Jewish *Targum* adds "in the pillar of cloud, and in the pillar of fire." It is a picture of God as the head of the Israelites, leading, guiding, and directing them through the wilderness from Egypt to Canaan. They had not been that way before, and even Moses admitted that he didn't know how to lead the people any farther than Mount Sinai, for that was as far as he had ever traveled in the wilderness. It became God's sole responsibility to move them from point A to point B; their responsibility began and ended in following His leadership. They didn't even have a voice or vote in that leadership. God chose the way, the time, the pace, and the campsite.

Nothing has changed, except that God is not geographically leading a great host of people; He is spiritually leading His Church from point A to point B. No amount of lusting for moving on will change our position, for unless God leads us we cannot make the smallest move. We've not been this way before, but God has, and He is leading His Sheep into green pastures.

In speaking of the shepherd, Jesus told His disciples, "When he putteth forth his own sheep, he goeth before them, and the sheep follow him: for they know his voice," and then Jesus added, "I am the good shepherd: the good shepherd giveth his life for the sheep" (John 10:4,11). God always goes before His people; He leads, not drives. We Westerners drive herds of sheep, often using clever dogs, but the Basque shepherds in Christ's day always led the sheep. God precedes His sheep to make preparation for them. He puts His life on the line in taking the risks first, facing the dangers, and finding a safe route through the lurking enemy. God can make a way where there seems to be no way, for He goes before His people, and when God arises, the enemies are scattered.

Christ's call to His disciples was consistently "Follow Me" (Matthew 4:19). The command was not "Go ye" (with one exception, following Christ's ascension) but "Follow Me." One of the pervading weaknesses on mission fields across the world is the overriding number of missionaries who were sent by the church rather than led by the Lord onto the field of service. God's work is performed through a partnership, not by proxy. God conducts His people; He does not merely consign them. We are being taken, not sent, into new territory with God. He chooses the place and He sets the pace, therefore the initiative is always God's, not ours. The responsibility and timing are His, and all necessary provisions are His provisions for us. Following God is not difficult compared to trying to precede him. All predetermining of our own paths and attempting to get God's approval is both difficult and dangerous. God goes *before*; we merely follow.

God Goes Through

The second thing David tells us about God's leading is that God goes through, for he said, ". . . when thou didst march through the wilderness" (verse 7). God not only goes before; He is going all the way. God did not merely lead Israel into the wilderness; He led them completely through it. This was Moses' point of argument with God when God threatened to destroy rebellious Israel and promised to begin a new nation with Moses. Moses reminded God that if He did this thing, the enemies around would always argue that God was great enough to get the people out of the bondage of Egypt, but He was not mighty enough to bring them into their inheritance (*see* Exodus 32:9–14). God accepted this argument of Moses and continued on as a guide for a people who were rebellious in their hearts toward Him.

God never leads His Church into a box canyon to abandon, to destroy, or to surrender her to an enemy. God always leads *out* in order to lead *into*. Deliverance *from* is never God's full purpose; He intends to deliver us *into* our inheritance. Whenever we succumb to that pernicious fear that God is going to abandon us, or that this is not the right place for us to be, we are living in open rebellion against the leadership God is trying to afford us. He knows where, when, how, and how much. Leadership is His job, and He is extremely good at it. He always goes through.

What a difference the wilderness experience is when we choose to go into the wilderness and when God leads us into the wilderness. When we choose the wilderness it seems to be endless, but when He leads us into the wilderness it is for a prescribed period of time. Israel had forty encampments in her forty years in the wilderness. Each was picked out by God and became a specific place of God's provision for all the people who had willingly followed Him into the new territory. While it may have seemed endless to the Israelites in the wilderness. God's timing had already predetermined an end.

If God goes *through* we can go through too. We used to sing Herbert Buffam's gospel song:

> I'm going through, Jesus, I'm going through;
> I'll pay the price whatever others do,
> I'll take the way with the Lord's anointed few;
> I'm going through, Jesus, I'm going through.

In today's generation there's a desperate need for the tenacity, dedication, and consecration that declares, "I have begun with God, and I will end with God." As is said of the 144,000 in heaven, ". . . These are they which follow the Lamb withersoever he goeth" (Revelation 14:4). The joy of being led by God is in the knowledge that it all "came to pass"; nothing came to stay.

God Overcomes Hindrances

Not one of us expects to follow God without hindrances, but David saw God completely overcoming hindrances, for he wrote, "The earth shook, the heavens also dropped at the presence of God: even Sinai itself was moved at the presence of God . . ." (Psalms 68:8). While this likely refers directly to the great physical phenomena displayed at the giving of the law at Sinai, Deborah spoke similarly of God after Israel's great victory over Sisera. She sang, "Lord, when thou wentest out of Seir, when thou marchedst out of the field of Edom, the earth trembled, and the heavens dropped, the clouds also dropped water. The mountains melted from before the Lord, even that Sinai from before the Lord God of Israel" (Judges 5:4,5). The experiences poetically referred to by both David and Deborah suggest at least three things about God's leading His people.

First of all, it is obvious that the presence of God causes the *earth* to respond to God's will. The Scriptures speak of the earth quaking, opening and closing, and crumbling at His command. When God leads His people through the earth He is in complete control of all the earthlies. Nothing catches Him unaware; nothing is beyond His control, and nothing is unavailable to His command. God even causes the earthlies to assist in bringing His people through into their inheritance. Paul told the church at Ephesus, "God has allowed us to know the secret of his plan, and it is this: he purposes in his sovereign will that all human history shall be consummated in Christ, that everything that exists in

Heaven or earth shall find its perfection and fulfilment in him. And here is the staggering thing – that in all which will one day belong to him we have been promised a share . . ." (Ephesians 1:9–11, PHILLIPS).

There is never a time in human history when the Church has a right to declare things to be out of control and detrimental to the plan of God, for God is in charge, and He knows what He is doing. Everything is controlled to help the Church come into her inheritance in God. Policital powers rise and fall, economies may alternately stimulate and stifle our life-style, and religious liberty may be given and then taken away, but none of it is beyond the control of God. All of it is in the scope of God's will, and all of it is for the sake of His Church. When Israel went through the land, God was in charge of the land, and He still is.

The presence of God causes the *heavens* to respond to His will. At Sinai the cloud and thick darkness dipped so low that the people lost sight of the mountain, and it seemed that it was going to engulf the whole congregation. It was an awesome experience, for out of the blackness of that cloud came piercing lightning and deafening thunder, both of which were superseded by the voice of God. To the people it seemed as though the heavens themselves had dropped to the earth.

We are caused to understand that the satanic realm now occupies the lower heavens – the atmosphere above us. When God begins to lead His people, even this satanic realm must cease hindering and start helping us get through into our inheritance. Just a few days out of Egypt, Israel stood fearfully all night as God opened the Red Sea for her to walk through. The dense cloud that separated them from the Egyptians was darkness to the enemy but light to God's people. When the chosen ones could not muster enough faith to walk throught he parted waters, God merely lifted the cloud, giving the Egyptians a clear shot at the Israelites. Although they could not have faith in God for deliverance, these Hebrews had great faith in the Egyptians' power for destruction, so they fled through the parted sea in the strength that the self-preservation instinct can give in a moment of extreme danger. Interestingly enough, the Book of Hebrews calls this entire process "faith" in saying, "By faith they passed through the Red Sea as by dry land . . ." (Hebrews 11:29). God caused the enemy to inspire faith in His people, and He still does. The lower heavens are available to God's command.

Furthermore, the third heaven, as Paul speaks of it, responds instantly to God's will. The angelic forces of the higher heavens are "ministering spirits, sent forth to minister for them who shall be heirs of salvation" (Hebrews 1:14). How little we realize that the angels are commissioned of God to protect, to provide, to give wisdom, and share understanding with the saints here on the earth. These angels are the messengers of God; they are the channels of communicating God's Word to us. Every angel God ever created is at the beck and call of God. Those angels that fell with Lucifer *must* do God's will and obey His command, and those that remain in His presence *delight* to do God's will at the slightest hint of His command. When God arises to lead His people through, all the help of heaven is at His command. We don't plead or command it, but if we need it God sends it.

The third thing that both David and Deborah sang about was that the presence of God causes the *legals* to bend at His will. "Sinai itself was moved at the presence of God . . ." is David's wording. Looking beyond the mountain itself to what happened on that mountain, we face the giving of the Law. Sinai consistently speaks of law. Not only will all the earthlies respond to God at His presence, and not only will all the heavenlies respond, but al the legals will bend to the presence of God. All of God's laws are subject to God's presence. Law was never intended to separate us from God; it is a schoolmaster to bring us into Christ, but too frequently law has been used as a club to terrorize or as a prison to incarcerate Christians. Religion often keeps men from moving to new locations with God through a rigid interpretation of the law, but if the law seems to hinder walking with God, God is greater than the law. He will not, of course, violate His own Word, but He does release us from the fear, condemnation, and penalty of the law, and He brings us into the liberty of Christ Jesus who fulfilled the entire law on our behalf. Now the law does not hinder; it helps us march on with God.

God Supplies Where He Leads

Not only does God overcome hindrances, but He is the perfect quartermaster – He supplies everything necessary for the march. David poetically puts it, "Thou, O God, didst send a plentiful rain . . ." (Psalms 68:9), but to this we must put the question, "When?" The Sacred Record does not chonicle one incident of rain from the moment Israel crossed the Red Sea until the second generation crossed the Jordan River into the Promised Land. It has been surmised that when that great cloud covered Sinai with its accompanying thunder and lightning, there must have been a thunderstorm at work over the camp, but if so, not one writer in the Bible ever mentions it. As a matter of fact, they seem to emphasize the sense of the supernatural in the cloud rather than a natural phenomenon.

To what, then, is David referring in speaking of a "plentiful rain"? Well, maybe he refers rather loosely to the constant supply of water that God gave them in the wilderness. There was the bitter water at Marah that God sweetened, there was the rock that gave forth water, and there was a well that sprang forth when the elders of Israel sang to it (see Numbers 21:17). Israel never lacked a water supply in her forty years of nomadic dwelling in the barren wilderness, but she never had a rainfall.

The Hebrew word translated here as "plentiful" is *nedabah*; for which Dr. Robert Young, in his *Analytical Concordance*, gives the meaning "a willing gift or offering." Accordingly, the Reverend A. R. Fausset, in his *Critical and Experimental Commentary on the Old Testament*, translates it "rain of liberalities." "Thou, O God, didst send a rain of liberalities." It is akin to Ezekiel's promise that "there shall be showers of blessings" (Ezekiel 34:26).

It is likely that David is referring to the manna, quail, water out of the rock, protection against the enemies, clothes that didn't wear out, and sundry other physical blessings and supplies that God lavishly poured out on Israel in the wilderness. That these temporal blessings were "plentiful," or a "rain of liberalities," is further underscored by the Hebrew word used for "send." It literally means "to shake out; to wave back and forwards so as to cause the rain of gracious gifts to fall on the whole people, and not merely on one favored section."

None would deny that God's Church has been blessed with a "rain of liberalities." We've had the "former and the latter rains" prophesied by Joel (2:23). We've received grace upon grace and have become the beneficiaries of gift after gift. God Himself loves us; Christ gave Himself for us, and the Holy Spirit lives within us. Surely these are "showers of blessings," or the "rain of liberalities." What God did for Israel in the wilderness He will do for His Church right now in these closing days of the history of the Church. "Every good gift and every perfect give is from above, and cometh down from the Father . . ." (James 1:17), and His gifts are characterized by sweetness, copiousness, and timeliness. He is a great Giver of gifts! He rains liberally upon His people.

Where God leads, God feeds. Where He guides, He provides. How many of God's servants have learned that God's program will never lack God's provision, for His will becomes my well of supply. Following God is never a walk into penury but a flight into plenty.

God Confirms His Leadings

A fifth factor in God's leadings which David mentions is that God confirms His leadings ". . . whereby thou didst confirm thine inheritance, when it was weary" (Psalms 68:9). When Moses convinced the children of Israel that God would lead them out of Egypt into the Promised Land, it sounded like a short walk, but, as the *Pulpit Commentary* (volume 9) suggests, "The wandering in the wilderness must have been inexpressibly dull and wearisome, especially to those who had left Egypt with the hope of a quick march through the waste, and a speedy entrance into a 'land flowing with milk and honey' (Exodus 3:17)." If God's only goal had been to get them out of Egypt into Canaan, He could have done it in three weeks or less, but God had a third goal that the people knew nothing about. He also wanted to get Egypt out of them, and that took a full forty years.

Israel had forty years of basic inactivity: no jobs; no heavy responsibilities; no fields to plow; no market to attend. Although she was moved forty times during these years, there isn't much excitement in being moved from one pile of rocks to another, or from one patch of sand to a larger patch of sand. It must have been boring much of the time.

Many of us have found the ways of the Lord to be pretty boring. There seem to be relentless repetition and stagnating sameness in the route He uses to get the world out of us in preparation to get us into our inheritance. It is little by little that God is changing us, but we want a lot of change all at once. God never argues with us; He merely leads us so far into the wilderness that we can't find our way back and then does His progressive work in our lives no matter how long it may take.

When our walk with God seems prosaic and stereotyped, and our Christian life becomes mediocre and monotonous. God mercifully confirms His leadings to assure us that He knows where we are, where we are going, and what time we will arrive. He uses His "rain of liberalities" to reassure us that He has neither forgotten nor forsaken us.

The Hebrew word David uses for "confirm" is *kûwn*, which is a primitive root meaning "to be erect" (that is, to stand perpendicular). It is often translated as "to establish or to prepare." As used here it signifies "to comfort, strengthen, cause to try again, or to lift from discouragement and despair."

When we are bowed down with discouragement, God causes us to stand erect, for He strengthens and comforts us with a fresh song in our spirits in the morning and a renewed sense that He has not withheld from us anything that is needful – and has actually given to us much that is luxurious. This confirms that God is not judging us; He is comfortingly confirming His will in our lives.

It is God's inheritance that He confirms, but what is God's inheritance? While Christ is the inheritance of the Church, it is Israel and the Church that are spoken of as God's inheritance, as Solomon reminded God in the prayer of dedication: "For thou didst separate them from among all the people of the earth, to be thine inheritance . . ." (1 Kings 8:53). We are God's inheritance, separated from the things of the earth to be participants in the things of God. We are His by creation, purchase, and love. Over and over again the Scriptures speak of us as being "His people; His sheep; His family; His Church; His Bride," and so forth.

Even though we are His inheritance – His people – we get weary with the burdensome rites of religion, with our own sins, with the sins of others, and with burdens of life that are heavy to carry. The temptations of satan and overt or subtle persecutions take their toll on our faith and strength. But God doesn't look down from heaven and cry, "Kill them. I want none but the strong in my procession." No, instead He confirms His weary inheritance with showers of blessings.

When God sees a weary pastor struggling with a stubborn congregation, He says, "Rain on him." When God sees an exhausted parishioner assailed by doubts and fears, He says "Rain on him." God comforts; He does not condemn. God blesses; He does not blame. God pours copiously of His mercy, of His love, of His goodness, of His grace, of His presence, of His power, of His life, of His fellowship – God rains upon His inheritance with His "rain of liberalities" in order to confirm, comfort, and cause His people to stand erect again with renewed courage and confidence.

God knows we get weary, and He knows that we oftentimes act stupidly when we are exhausted, so He doesn't answer too many "weary prayers"; He just rains on us to bring us back to spiritual vigor very much as a shower can cause drooping flowers to stand erect once more.

By God's Word and God's Spirit He refreshes the weary ones. We may get weary *in* the way, but we should not allow ourselves to get tired *of* the way. There is rest for the weary, peace for the troubled, health for the sick, and hope for the discouraged, but there is nothing available for the dropout. If we get so weary we don't know how we can go on, we should wisely sit down and wait for the next shower of blessings. The Lord will yet encourage us; the Lord will yet strengthen us; He will comfort us; He will yet lift us up by sending either an angel or a member of the Body of Christ to "confirm His inheritance."

Rest in the Lord, but don't run from the Lord. We are allowed times of ease while following God, but we dare not seek an easier way than God's way, for there is no easier route. God always brings us the easiest way we are willing to come, no matter how rough it may be at times. Those who seek their own way always end up at a dead end, and they are amazed how far back it is into the ways of the Lord. Just ask the prodigal son.

God Arrives With Us

Finally, David assures us that God arrives with us! "Thy congregation hath dwelt therein: thou, O God, has prepared of thy goodness for the poor" (Psalms 68:10). The "poor" must refer to the once homeless Israelites in the wilderness as well as to the present pilgrims who are in between Egypt and Canaan. God has prepared a home for them.

The *congregation* in the Hebrew literally means "host". God does not begin with a great host of people and finally lead only a few people into their inheritance. If God begins with a "host" He will arrive with a "host." Paul declared that he was "confident of this very thing, that he which hath begun a good work in you will perform it until the day of Jesus Christ" (Philippians 1:6). It will not be the "select of the elect" that come through; it will be those who have followed God's leadership whether filled with elation or exhaustion. God is going to get us through!

The word *therein* obviously has to refer to Canaan, for the Promised Land was the object for which they marched through the wilderness. God declares that this poor, homeless group of chosen people are going to get into the promises that motivated them to forsake a former way of life. God is a convenant-keeping God; a God who cannot violate His word; a God who has ". . . magnified thy word above all thy name" (Psalms 138:2). If He promises, He will perform.

Furthermore, it declares that God prepares ahead for our arrival – ". . . thou, O God, hast prepared thy goodness for the poor" (verse 10). We don't wander through the wilderness and stumble into the land to begin carving out something for ourselves; God has already prepared everything we need before our arrival. As surely as Israel found houses, wells, crops, and cattle awaiting them in Canaan, so we will find all needful things awaiting our arrival in our land of promises. Jesus assured us, ". . . I go to prepare a place for you" (John 14:2).

God is a perfect Guide. He arrives at the proper destination every time. He never gets lost, and He never loses a "wagon train" to "Indians." He gets every host of people through to the promises made to them. We who are His inheritance are safely led into our inheritance.

The prophet Isaiah understood this principle, for he wrote, "And the Lord shall guide thee continually, and satisfy thy soul in drought, and make fat thy bones. . . . And they that shall be of thee shall build the old waste places: thou shalt raise up the foundations of many generations; and thou shalt be called, The repairer of the breach, The restorer of paths to dwell in" (Isaiah 58:11,12). We shall yet arrive in our inheritance if we follow the Lord, but it will not be without warfare, for there are enemies in the land that must be driven out. Praise the Lord that God is not only a Leader; He is also a Warrior who has never lost a battle.

4
God Warring

The Lord gave the word: great was the company of those that published it. Kings of armies did flee apace; and she that tarried at home divided the spoil. Though ye have lien among the pots, yet shall ye be as the wings of a dove covered with silver, and her feathers with yellow gold. When the Almighty scattered kings in it, it was white as snow in Salmon.

PSALMS 68:11-14

The proclamation "Let God arise" or "God is already beginning to arise" may challenge God's Church to follow Him into new territory, but to the enemies who occupy the territory into which God is going to lead us, that cry is tantamount to a declaration of war.

Every bit of territory into which God leads His people is already occupied, and we gain new territory not merely by walking into it but by warring in it. Our march with God is a conquer-and-occupy operation. We are always contested when we enter into our inheritance in God. As long as we remain in the wilderness we are left pretty much alone, for it is uninhabited until we get there, but when we cross our Jordans and set foot into the Land of Promise toward which God has been faithfully leading us over a protracted period of time, we will not only find houses, harvests, and honey, but we will come face-to-face with the occupants of those houses, the sowers of those harvests, and the owners of the beehives. They are not giving us this land as a present; God is giving it to us as an inheritance. Taking God's gift out of their hand will entail a conflict.

We do well to remind ourselves that we are not taking away from the enemy anything that belongs to him; we are merely unseating a usurper or removing a squatter from his illegal residence. All territory into which God leads us belongs to the Church. In Israel's case, God was only bringing them back to territory that had been given to Abraham but lost to his progeny during their long stay in Egypt. This land was their land, the wells had been dug by their forefathers, and God was leading Israel to repossess her inheritance in God.

Happily, this is God's war, not ours. As God spoke to Jehoshaphat He speaks to the Church: ". . . the battle is not yours, but God's. . . . Ye shall not need to fight in this battle: set yourselves, stand ye still, and see the salvation of the Lord with you . . ." (2 Chronicles 20:15,17). Since God's method of warfare is so different from ours, we do well to consider His tactics and methods of conquest on behalf of His Church.

God's War Zone

Sometimes Christians fail to realize that there are at least three war zones, or three areas of life, in which heaven's forces engage satan's army in conflict. Each war zone is territory that belongs to the saints by right of divine gift and by right of our inheritance in Jesus Christ. We know that sin cost man his access to heaven, this authority on the earth, and the control of his own heart and life, and this territory needs to be repossessed and reactivated by the saints, both individually and collectively. God's gifts are never withdrawn, but we sometimes sell our birthright or succumb to the intimidation of an enemy usurper. Either way we may lose possession of what is rightfully ours, and, as we are so often reminded, possession is nine points of the law.

The armies who fought with Joshua spent a lifetime repossessing what God had given to Abraham. They had been told, "Every place that the sole of your foot shall tread upon, that have I given unto you, as I said unto Moses" (Joshua 1:3). They possessed the land not by a statement of their faith but by the step of their feet. Only as they walked in was the enemy driven out. God had explained to Moses, "I will not drive them out from before thee in one year, lest the land become desolate, and the beast of the field multiply against thee. By little and little I will drive them out from before thee, until thou be increased, and inherit the land" (Exodus 23:29–30).

Just as Israel was led to conquer Canaan at a rate she was prepared to occupy, so God leads His saints to conquer what they are willing and able to possess. It is not instant victory but persistent conquest into which we have been called. Quite frankly, the rate at which we possess our inheritance is determined more by our willingness to occupy what we conquer than by God's ability to conquer the territory for us. It is dangerous to conquer land we are unwilling to control or occupy, for the usurper will circle behind us and reinhabit it, leaving us with an enemy before and behind us.

Every bit of territory that God enabled us to conquer in the past He expects us to maintain into eternity. In the wilderness we forsook one campsite to move into the next, but in the Promised Land we do not abandon; we annex. We are not exchanging territory; we are expanding into new territory so that the old and the new are combined into one. This is far more than a conquest; it is a colonization. Therefore it cannot be a three-day war, and it is far more a three-front war.

The first war zone in which God wars is heaven itself. We seem to understand from the Scriptures that there are three heavens. The first heaven is our atmosphere, the second heaven is sidereal space, and the third heaven is God's abode. It was in this third heaven, the abode of God, that

Lucifer insurrected and introduced sin into God's creation. When he was cast out he came down to earth (*see* Revelation 12:12) to become "the prince of the power of the air, the spirit that now worketh in the children of disobedience" (Ephesians 2:2). This first heaven, the atmosphere above us, is under satanic control, and we must go through that territory to reach God in the higher, or "third," heavens (*see* Corinthians 12:2). This explains some of the difficulty we have in prayer, especially in the early beginnings of a prayer time. We are seeking to traverse through inhabited territory, and we are being contested,

In the Old Testament, Jacob received a vision wherein he saw a ladder of access to the third heaven piercing right through this first heaven, and on that ladder he saw angels of God ascending and descending upon the earth (*see* Genesis 28:12). In the New Testament, when Nathanael came to Jesus he was told, "Verily, verily, I say unto you, Hereafter ye shall see heaven open, and the angels of God ascending and descending upon the Son of man" (John 1:51). Jacob's ladder turns out to be our Lord. Our route of access to God through the satanic realm is through Jesus Christ, God's Son. It is a battlefield, but Christ pierced a neutral zone all the way through it at His ascension after His resurrection. We Christians do not war in this zone; it is an angelic conflict waged on our behalf. We merely enter into the divine victory that has been gained for us.

A second war zone, or a second front in this warfare of conquest, is the earth itself. Israel was concerned with earthly territory and fought earthly powers, and the Church is often opposed by earthly powers, whether political, economic, religious, or physical. Church history shows how bloody this conflict has often been, but it also reveals that "the earth is the Lord's and the fulness thereof" (Psalms 24:1). God still reigns in our earthly realm and is able to control all forces for the benefit of His Church here on the earth. Daniel said of God that "He changeth the times and the seasons: he removeth kings, and setteth up kings . . ." (Daniel 2:21), while Asaph declared, "For promotion cometh neither from the east, nor from the west, nor from the south. But God is the judge: he putteth down one, and setteth up another" (Psalms 75:6,7). The hearts of the saints need not be fearful when looking at the things that are happening here on the earth, for they are all under our heavenly Father's control; this is still our Father's world. Saints should never give up their inheritance rights to the earth. We are not called to fold our hands and wait until we get to heaven, for we are already on Daddy's territory. He owns this farm. The cattle on a thousand hills belongs to the Lord, the hills under those cattle belong to the Lord, and the gold and silver under those hills are His also. This is my Father's world!

There are times when the sharecroppers and usurper-princes who inhabit this world come up against the saints, declaring that we have no rights, possess no authority, and can wield no power because we are seen as a small minority. But we do have rights, authority and power, for this is Dad's home; it is our land, and we'll do things God's way. The hearts of the saints need not be fearful when looking at the things that are happening here on the earth, for they are under our heavenly Father's control, and it is His will to ultimately restore ownership of this world to the Church, including her authorities over nations and creation.

It is healthy for us to be reminded that ". . . For we wrestle not against flesh and blood, but against principalities, against powers, against the rulers of the darkness of this world, against spiritual wickedness in high places" (Ephesians 6:12; see also 2 Corinthians 10:4). Even here in the earthly war zone it is a spiritual battle.

The third front in which we find ourselves engaged in conflict, or the third war zone, is the human heart. Each of us is far more engaged in this conflict than in the other two put together, for most of the time it is the soul/spirit of man in which heaven and hell are locked in mortal combat. It is a battle for the human mind and will.

Eve's temptation was not coercion or even bribery; it was persuasion. It was her mind that was assailed; it was her will that was sought. When we come to the New Testament to watch the temptation of Christ, we see, again, that it was gentle persuasion that the devil used. The tempter wanted Jesus to turn His will from the Father to the fugitive from the Father, satan. The forty-days temptation in the wilderness was a battle of the mind and will, for the ultimate purpose of all temptation is to cause us to violate the will of God. Satan would love to have us surrender to his will, but he is satisfied if he can at least cause us to violate God's will; hence if we exert our will against God's will, satan has accomplished his primary purpose. He has, at this point, frustrated God's will, and he is satisfied, because the moment we begin to operate in our will we have weakened the authority of the Church in both our lives and in the world in general.

When Paul said, "For the weapons of our warfare are not carnal, but mighty through God to the pulling down of strong holds" he added, "Casting down imaginations, and every high thing that exalteth itself against the knowledge of God, and bringing into captivity every thought to the obedience of Christ" (2 Corinthians 10:4,5). The operation of every divine weapon is against the thought life; they come to the mind, for here is where the battle is engaged. Yet how frequently we lose sight of this seemingly obvious truth. While we await the enemy's frontal attack with tanks and bazookas, he approaches us with an idea, a criticism, a complaint, a moment of self-pity, or a doubt, none of which seems demonic or dangerous at the moment. If, instead, he should approach us with the charge that Jesus is not the Son of the Most High God, we would recognize it as a satanic attack and would declare war on it, but as long as it is but a suggestion to the mind we tend to think that it is our own thought pattern and give lodging to the dangerous weapon in our soul.

No, satan rarely makes a frontal attack on the saints; he comes on far more subtly than that. He has an uncanny ability to find our area of weakness and direct our minds to skepticism, discouragement, uncertainty, cynicism, or apathy without our even realizing that a war is going on between God's way and satan's way – and that it is being fought in our thought patterns. How we need to be aware of the difference between criticism of circumstances and a spiritual conflict exploding in our minds. Only the naive would deny the reality of an active spiritual warfare as they follow God. Our confusion is not whether there is a war, but where it is.

God's Weapon

If the conflict in which we are engaged is not physical, then the weapons used cannot be physical either. In displaying God warring, David described His weapons as "the Lord gave the word . . ." (Psalms 68:11). In the Keil-Delitzsch *Commentary on the Old Testament* Franz Delitzsch, the great German Lutheran theologian, translates this portion of the verse as, "The Lord will sound forth the mandate . . ." (volume 5). The Hebrew word used here for this mandate and translated "word" in the King James Bible is *omer*, and it is translated as "word" only twice in the entire Bible. Franz Delitzsch says that "it always denotes an important utterance, more particularly God's word of promise, or His word of power, which is represented elsewhere as a mighty voice of thunder, or a trumpet-blast."

God's fundamental weapon is His mandate, His Word of power. When God thunders from heaven, all hell trembles, all creation responds obediently, and all Christians should humble themselves to instant obedience, for God's Word carries in it the power to perform; it is a creative word against which nothing can prevail. It is far more than the weak preaching we so carelessly declare to be the Word of God, and it is infinitely above the prophetic utterances mere man may speak. David tried to give poetic expression to the effective working of the voice of God when he wrote, "The voice of the Lord is upon the the waters: the God of glory thundereth. . . . The voice of the Lord is powerful; the voice of the Lord is full of majesty. The voice of the Lord breaketh the cedars. . . . The voice of the Lord divideth the flames of fire. The voice of the Lord shaketh the wilderness . . ." (Psalms 29:3,4,5,7,8). This voice is God's number-one weapon.

Having declared that "the Lord gave the word," David adds, "great was the company of those that published it" (Psalms 68:11). In a way wonderful to God and mysterious to man, after God speaks His mandate, or creative Word, He uses redeemed humans to proclaim that word. God cries it from heaven, and we cry it on earth. There are those rare occasions throughout the Scriptures where God spoke directly from heaven, and it was generally interpreted as thunder by the masses of people, but most of His speaking has been through human channels. God's proclamation comes through persons. Paul wrote, ". . . it pleased God by the foolishness of preaching to save them that believe" (1 Corinthians 1:21). We must always distinguish between preaching foolishness and the foolishness of preaching, of course! When man is engaged in declaring God's proclamation he becomes a second weapon in God's arsenal, for God chooses to speak to men through men. That's why He became a man in Jesus. Men don't hear God – they are usually tuned to the wrong channel – but people hear people, so God speaks through them.

The Hebrew word for "company" in this verse is *tsaba* and it is in the feminine voice. The Amplified Bible translates this verse: "The Lord gives the word [of power]; the women who bear and publish (the news) are a great host," while Franz Delitzsch translates it, ". . . Of the women who herald victory there is a great army" (*Commentary on the Old Testament*, volume 5). He then comments, "God's decisive word shall go forth this time, and of the evangelists, like Miriam and Deborah, there shall be a great host."

In *Clarke's Commentary* (volume 3), Adam Clarke writes, " 'Of the female preachers there was a great host.' Such is the literal translation of this passage; the reader may make of it what he pleases. Some think it refers to the *women* who, with music, songs, and dances, celebrated the victories of the Israelites over their enemies. But the publication of *good news*, or of any *joyful event*, belonged to *the women*. It was they who announced it to the people at large; and to this universal custom, which prevails to the *present day*, the psalmist alludes."

For years there has been biased debate as to whether women can be preachers of the Word, but once God has said a thing anyone has the right to repeat it. We all can be proclaimers of this good news. That is what we have been commissioned to proclaim – good news – for the Gospel means "good news."

We are not called to proclaim the dirty, filthy powers of sin and satan; we deal with redemption from the dirty, filthy powers of sin, and redemption is good news! We have been sent not to expose sin but to expound a Saviour. Our proclamation is that Christ has conquered sin, satan, death, and hell. We have good news to share, and this good news is God's mighty weapon whether declared from God in heaven or by the saints here on the earth.

God's Warriors

It is easy, and in some religious circles it is even popular, to see the Church as God's mighty army doing battle against the satanic kingdom, but I believe David is far more accurate, for he writes, "The chariots of God are twenty thousand, even thousands of angels . . ." (Psalms 68:17). God's Word of *power* is heralded by His angels. We mortals are too puny to be able to handle such power; at best we merely report the Word after it has been uttered. Even the law was given by the mediacy of the angels, according to Acts 7:53 and Galatians 3:19. One of the few accounts of a spiritual war actually being fought is recorded by John when he wrote, "And there was war in heaven: Michael and his angels fought against the dragon; and the dragon fought and his angels, And prevailed not; neither was their place found any more in heaven. And the great dragon was cast out, that old serpent, called the Devil, and Satan, which deceiveth the whole world: he was cast out into the earth, and his angels were cast out with him (Revelation 12:7–9).

Who is in conflict here? Angels! God did not contest satan; Michael and his angels did. It wouldn't even be a fair war if God locked in mortal combat with satan, for they are not even on the same plane of creation. This great war in heaven was between God's faithful archangel, Michael, and His faithless anointed cherub, Lucifer. Their conflict was not with mighty thunderbolts, or awesome spiritual weapons about which we know nothing; this was a forensic battle – a debate – a war of words. John says, "And they overcame him . . . by the word of their testimony" (Revelation 12:11). This battle was fought as two attorneys would contend in a court of law, or as two debaters would dispute on a debate team. It is not using weapons to kill the opponent; it is using words to control the opponent, and Michael had the Word of God, while Lucifer had only his own word; and God's Word always prevails. From that day to this God's angels have been able to keep Lucifer, the devil, satan, the accuser, or whatever title you prefer, under control by using nothing more or less than God's Word. God's Word is a mighty word; it is an authoritative word.

The conflict has always been God's declared Word countered by satan's arguments. Consistently, when God's special messengers, the angels, assert God's Word of *power*, there is not enough force in hell to stand against it. Hell is on very shaky legal grounds anyway. Satan claims it as his own, while God declares it to be divine territory reserved for punishment. Satan can often outtalk man, but he has never successfully outtalked God or God's angelic messengers. Since satan's only remaining power this side of the cross is the power of persuasion, he is at a great disadvantage in spiritual warfare, for he has never persuaded God of anything. God cannot be deceived, coerced, bribed, or outmanoeuvred.

Although I earnestly contend that spiritual warfare is a forensic contest between angels of God and angels of Lucifer, I must, in all honesty, admit that God's redeemed do sometimes get into this conflict, not as soldiers in the army, but as witnesses in the court of law or as proclaimers of God's Word. When we say what God has said, to that extent, at least, we are involved in the warfare. But we are never originators of a contesting word; we are merely proclaimers.

I strongly recommend against initiating any battle against the satanic kingdom, but when God has made His proclamation – when the Word is trumpeted in heaven, earth, and hell, "Let God arise, let his enemies be scattered . . ." (Psalms 68:1) – and we know that as we move into new territory there will be legal battles to be fought and an enemy to be conquered, then all ages, maturity levels, sexes, and cultures become participants in this end of the battle. We proclaim the name of the Lord. Often we proclaim the victory of our God in the face of the enemy before he has retreated one step. We declare that he has no legal grounds on which to stand because God's Word is contrary to every position he has taken. We let the powers of opposition know that they cannot successfully withstand us since God is *leading us* into the territory; He is *not merely sending us* in. We do not go as God's advance guard; we are His rearward. We are coming behind Him, picking up the spoils.

Actually, we are far more war correspondents than warriors. We communicate, not combat. We are at the battlefront recording and subsequently reporting what God and His angels are doing to the enemy. It is God's Word that is producing; our word is but a proclamation of that production. Nothing we say disturbs the devil very much, but everything that God says becomes law by which the devil must live. If we are called upon to be a momentary participant in God's war, our role is little more than to announce, "Father says . . ."

God, the Winner!

God allows us to go along with Him in some of the warfare as a correspondent, and great is the company of those who are heralding to heaven, earth, and hell, "God is winning! God's winning! New territory has just been conquered."

This exuberant host proclaims the victories of God in praise, in song, in dance, in instrumental playing, in singing together and singing separately, in clapping, and in shouting. Those who remember V-E Day at the end of World War II and the subsequent surrender of Japan can recall the tremendous jubilation that was released in the cities of the world. Noise, shouting, hugging, singing, waving of flags and banners, impromptu parades, and all-night parties were everywhere. After a long and bitter conflict we heard the announcement, "Victory," and our joy knew no bounds. Should not the Lord's people also be jubilant as they proclaim the victories of our God throughout the world?

He is victorious, you know. God is always triumphant. David declared, "Kings of armies did flee apace . . ." (Psalms 68:12), but the Hebrew demands a repetition: "did flee; did flee." The Amplified Bible translates it, "The kings of the enemies' armies, they flee, they flee!"

Most spiritual battles are short-lived. When God's angels engage satan's angels in battle, the proclaimed Word of the Lord is a producing Word that causes the enemy to flee. How can the enemy army stand against God's Word when it is being enforced by God's angels? God's Word will always prevail. You cannot find one passage in the Bible where God ever lost a battle. Oh, you will find a few places where He never showed up and let His sinning people lose to their enemies as a chastisement, but wherever God was present He was victorious. God's army has never lost a war!

It is likely that all of us have been in some battles where we lost to the enemy, but a post mortem will reveal that we did not use God's weapons. Whenever a conflict begins in our mind, and we try to use our mind instead of God's Word to fight this war in our mind, we have already lost the battle, for we are no match for satan's reasoning. He has been around far longer than we have. He knows God and the heavenlies on an experiential level; we know it more theologically and practically. We can't even match the devil in religion, for he is a very religious being and knows far more about religion than we do. But when we use the weapons that Michael in heaven and Jesus on earth used – "it is written" – we cannot lose the conflict, for we are declaring divine law to which satan must be subject.

It is not our words, or even the words of the Church, that cause satan to give up the conflict and yield territory to the saints; it is the legal Word of God spoken by one who knows it is God's Word and whose life is submitted to that Word. Don't try to battle satan into submission with a Word to which you are not personally submitted, for then you are back to a clashing of the minds again. It is that portion of God's Word that has become life to you that becomes death to him. The moment we declare, "God's Word says . . ." the enemy retorts with, "Hath God said?" At that moment we had better be able to prove by our lives that we know God has said it. That is no time for weak theology, inaccurate quoting of the Scripture, or the mere singing of a song.

When the Word is proclaimed by the angels, or by faith-filled, Bible-believing saints, the enemy flees. Both Peter and James tell us to resist the devil, and James assures us that the devil will flee from us (*see* James 4:7 and 1 Peter 5:8,9). God never flees before anyone. It is the devil who flees. It is rebellious men who flee. It is stubborn saints who flee, for the awesome power of God's Word will drive all opposition from the presence of God.

God's Winnings

God is not only the winner, but there are some spoils. David said, ". . . and she that tarried at home divided the spoil" (Psalms 68:12). We are consciously aware that the spoil belongs to the victor, but are we equally aware that the spoil also belongs to the victor's wife? When the warrior comes back from battle he brings his booty with him. No wonder, then, that the women so joyously proclaim the victory, for it means that they will share in the gold and silver, the earrings and bracelets, and garments of rare beauty.

It is certainly consistent with the Scripture that the spoils of God's wars are shared with his wife, the Church, for what the Father has promised the Son, Christ has, in turn, shared with the Church. The prophet said, "Therefore will I divide him a portion with the great, and he shall divide the spoil with the strong . . ." (Isaiah 53:12). The Church is a beneficiary of the booty along with Christ as she enters into a share of the winnings of war.

What has been snatched from the usurper has been distributed to the saints. God wins the hearts of men, and the Church gets them as converts. God pulls down strongholds over a city, and the Church enters into a great spiritual freedom. God liberates men from inner bondages, and the Church shares in the jubilation of a newfound freedom.

Peace is a spoil of war enjoyed by all whether they served in the army or not. Joy is also a spoil of war, one into which far too few modern Christians have entered. Security is a spoil of war, as are comfort and family relationships. All of this is a gift God shares with His Church. He conquered the enemy on our behalf, and all the spoils of that conquest are available to His Church. It is no wonder, then, that Paul exclaimed, "Now thanks be to God, which always causeth us to triumph in Christ . . ." (2 Corinthians 2:14).

God's army always defeats satan's forces and brings home the spoils. These we share not by right of our conquest but as a result of our relationship. "She that tarried at home divided the spoil," David says. Being a participant in God's hoard requires being a resident in God's house. We must share the same home if we would share what is His. But just where is God's dwelling?

5
God Dwelling

The hill of God is as the hill of Bashan; an high hill as the hill of Bashan. Why leap ye, ye high hills? this is the hill which God desireth to dwell in; yea, the Lord will dwell in it for ever. The chariots of God are twenty thousand, even thousands of angels: the Lord is among them, as in Sinai, in the holy place. Thou hast ascended on high, thou hast led captivity captive: thou hast received gifts for men; yea, for the rebellious also, that the Lord God might dwell among them.

PSALMS 68:15–18

The cry "Let God arise" always signified a march – change was about to continue – but because of promise Israel knew that they would not be pilgrims forever; their ultimate home was the Promised Land. Progressively, Psalm Sixty-eight takes us from the wanderings of the wilderness to the conquest of Canaan. By this point in the psalm, warfare is over; perhaps Israel would no longer hear the cry "Let God arise."

But what about God? Would He forsake them now that they were in the land? Would their permanent dwellings cost them the personal presence of the God who had led them so victoriously to their present position of peace and plenty?

Mere observation indicates that this question has been asked by many groups of Christians since the days of Moses and David. Led out of sin or religious hypocrisy by God's presence, they enjoyed the provisions and presence of God throughout the days of their struggles and nomadic wanderings. But when they colonized into a church and grew into a denomination, they wondered if the presence of God would remain among them. How fearful some groups have been even to construct a quality meeting place for their church because the presence of God had been so evident among them while they met in private homes and rented buildings. Somehow they equated the transient and temporary with the divine presence and radiant glory.

The key to God's presence is not rented versus constructed church facilities, nor is it in the form or style of worship. God desires to dwell among His people on a permanent basis and would joyfully bring those people into a permanent habitation. Our only danger of losing the divine presence lies in our attitudes, for whenever we become independent of God in our attitudes, God's presence departs. If structure, community, and numerical strength cause us to feel self-sufficient, then God may very well seek another group with whom to dwell, but if we maintain our awareness of our need for God, it is His good pleasure to bring us into the land of promise and place us in permanent houses.

In retrospect, David could give a threefold answer to this unspoken query, "Where will God dwell now that we are in the land?" Each of David's answers assures us that God purposes to dwell among His people perpetually, regardless of their circumstances, stations in life, or positions on the earth.

Gods Dwells Among His Church on the Earth

The first locale of God's presence, David suggests to us, is called "the hill of God" (Psalms 68:15). Earlier, David had written, "Who shall ascend into the hill of the Lord?" (Psalms 24:3), and in both places he is referring to Zion, the hill in Jerusalem upon which the Temple was constructed. It is likely that remembrance of Israel's victory over the kings of the Gentiles inspired the poet with joyful assurance that Zion is the inaccessible dwelling place of Elohim, the God of the heavenly hosts.

Throughout the Old Testament, Zion was seen as the habitation of God, and whether the allusion was to the city of Jerusalem or to the Temple in Jerusalem, it was always seen as a sacred and holy place. In the *Zondervan Pictorial Encyclopedia of the Bible* A. A. MacRae observes, "But since Zion is thus 'the joy of all the earth' (Psalms 48:2 cf. Isaiah 18:7), it became synonymous with redemption as occurring in any nation; accordingly, to know God and to be written in His book is equated in the Psalms with being 'born in Zion' (Psalms 87:4–6). It suggests Isaiah's description of the elect of God as 'every one who has been recorded for life in Jerusalem' (Isaiah 4:3). In apostolic usage Mt. Zion (Sion, KJV) comes to represent 'the city of the living God, the heavenly Jerusalem' " (Hebrews 12:22).

Because much of what is said about Zion is equally said of the Church, it is quite easy to see Zion as an Old Testament euphemism for the Church, or at the very least, a beautiful type and example of the Church for which Jesus Christ died. God dwells in "the hill of God . . ."; He dwells in Zion; God dwells in His Church. Throughout the New Testament a variety of plural nouns is used to describe the Church. It is called "the body of Christ" (1 Corinthians 12:27); "the household of God" (Ephesians 2:19); "an habitation of God through the Spirit" (Ephesians 2:22); the family of God (Ephesians 3:15); "a spiritual house" (1 Peter 2:5), and "a holy nation" (1 Peter 2:9), just to name a few of the most common expressions. All of these pictures of the Church speak of God dwelling, abiding, remaining, inhabiting, residing or living among His people, the Church.

The Church is far more than God's representative here on the earth; she is His embassy in this world – His earthly residence, His place of abode. The Church is the Holy of Holies in the earthly tabernacle. Therefore, the Ark of the

Lord with its attached Mercy Seat is in the Church, not in the world. The voice of the Lord, which always spoke from between the faces of the Cherubim on that Mercy Seat, is also in the Church, not in the capitals of the world system. The universal Church of the Lord Jesus Christ is vested with the presence of the Living God. "The Lord hath chosen Zion; he hath desired it for his habitation," the psalmist said (Psalms 132:13).

Here in Psalm Sixty-eight God's Zion is colorfully contrasted with the world's Bashan: "The hill of God is as the hill of Bashan; an high hill as the hill of Bashan" (Psalms 68:15). Geographically, Bashan is a many-peaked mountain, called by some "a mountain range." It is volcanic and basalt in composition, and has towers, columns, cliffs, and rugged, sharp points. It so contrasts with little limestone Zion, which hardly qualifies for the word *hill*, much less *mountain*. In his *Critical and Experimental Commentary* A. R. Fausset suggests, "There was a peculiar propriety, from its (Bashan) position on the boundary between Judea and the heathen world, in employing it as a symbol of the world's might" (volume 3).

One of the few battles that Moses led the children of Israel in fighting was the battle of Endrei against Og, king of Bashan (*see* Numbers 21:33), so Bashan was obviously enemy territory. In this Sixty-eighth Psalm David used Bashan as a poetic emblem of world kingdoms, which often look like impenetrable fortresses towering loftily over the Church of God. Little do these Bashans of this world realize that their greatness is only by the grace of God, and that God ignores the mighty things of this world and chooses to dwell with lowly little Zion.

This world may be a high place and a stronghold of the enemy, but God dwells in His Church right in the midst of this Bashan. God does not fear or ignore the enemy – He moves into His territory and chooses a hill to dwell in. In the midst of godliness, idolatry, humanism, and paganism, God dwells in His Church, which has not been taken out of the world but kept in the midst of the world, for in His high priestly prayer Jesus told the Father, "I pray not that thou shouldest take them out of the world, but that thou shouldest keep them from the evil. They are not of the world, even as I am not of the world" (John 17:15,16).

This coexistence of God in the Church may afford security to God's Church, but it produces perpetual insecurity to the world system, for "Bashan" is perpetually jealous of "Zion." "Why leap ye, ye high hills? this is the hill which God desireth to dwell in; yea, the Lord will dwell in it for ever" (Psalms 68:16), David wrote. Our King James translation might cause us to think that Bashan was reacting jubilantly to God's presence in Zion, but Jerome translates this passage as "Why do ye look with suspicion?" In Arabic it means "to watch against, to lay snare," so it is not happiness that causes the high hills to leap. The Modern Language translation of the Bible handles this verse as "Why do you gaze with envious hostility, O many-peaked mountains, at the mountains which God has chosen for His abode?" while the Living Bible says, "Well may you look with envy at Mount Zion, the mount where God has chosen to live forever."

This "leaping" of which David speaks is with envious desire of devastating the hill which God loves, and the setting up of themselves above it. Satan has never turned from his original desire to be above God; he wants to rule and be worshipped, and hence he causes the world system, over which he exerts a strong controlling influence, to also yearn to lord it over God's Church. Envious of our peace, jealous of our warm family relationships, condemned by our morality, and frustrated by God's presence among us, the world seeks occasion to "leap" the Church in an endeavor to crush her and blot out her existence from the earth. On occasion this has taken the form of warfare, imprisonment, and severe persecution. At other times, and in other places, it is less overt, but it is insidious, insistent, and intense.

But these high mountains are nothing before God. God's Church is built upon a rock, and Jesus insisted that "the gates of hell shall not prevail against it" (Matthew 16:18). The world sees the Church as an impotent minority locked into an old-fashioned morality. They tell our young people that the Church is out of step with reality, and that it holds no authoritative place in our society. But Daniel saw a small stone cut out of the mountain without hands, and he watched that stone become a great mountain filling the whole earth, both breaking in pieces and consuming the kingdoms in it (*see* Daniel 2:34,35).

In a much earlier psalm, David wrote:

> Why do the heathen rage, and the people imagine a vain thing? The kings of the earth set themselves, and the rulers take counsel together against the Lord, and against his anointed, saying, Let us break their bands asunder, and cast away their cords from us. He that sitteth in the heavens shall laugh: the Lord shall have them in derision. Then shall he speak unto them in his wrath, and vex them in his sore displeasure. Yet have I set my king upon my holy hill of Zion.
>
> PSALMS 2:1-6

God dwells in Zion; God dwells in His Church. No amount of jealousy, wrath, or rage on the part of the world system can keep God from inhabiting His church. In His timing God intends that the Church shall possess all the kingdoms of this world, for Daniel wrote, "But the saints of the most High shall take the kingdom, and possess the kingdom for ever, even for ever and ever" (Daniel 7:18).

God Dwells Among His Angels

"The chariots of God are twenty thousand . . ." David wrote (Psalms 68:17). The Reverend A. R. Fausset says, "The *chariots* are put for *those who rode in them*. To show the infinite security of God's people, the *Myriad* is doubled – '*two* myriads' " (*Critical and Experimental Commentary,* volume 3). While this is very likely true, the use of the word *chariot* for what is obviously the action of God's angels is not totally foreign to the Scripture. When Elijah was taken up into heaven, his servant, Elisha, saw ". . . a chariot of fire, and horses of fire, and parted them both asunder; and Elijah went up by a whirlwind into heaven" (2 Kings 2:11). Many years later when Elisha was trapped in the city of Dothan, completely surrounded by the Syrians, his servant panicked. Calmly, "Elisha prayed, and said, Lord, I pray thee, open his eyes, that he may see. And the Lord opened the eyes of the young man; and he saw: and, behold, the mountain was full of horses and chariots of fire round about Elisha" (2 Kings 6:17).

So David is not taking poetic license in referring to God's angels as "chariots." This is the way others had seen them. God's war chariots of the heavenly hosts are collectively called angels. They are the strength and protection of the Lord's people. In referring to them as chariots, David pictures their swiftness in doing God's work. They are the chariots of God in which He rides about the world doing His will. They are the chariots in which Christ ascended to heaven, and in which He will descend again at the last day. It is likely that these angel chariots are used when the Lord now gathers the souls of His people to Himself at the time of death, and they will probably be the agents at the resurrection of the just when their bodies are raised by God, for "Are they [angels] not all ministering spirits, sent forth to minister for them who shall be heirs of salvation?" (Hebrews 1:14).

The number of these angels that are available to the service of God is staggering. "The chariots of God are twenty thousand, even thousands of angels," David wrote (Psalms 68:17). I am told that the Hebrew construction is literally "thousands, and again thousands, numberless, incalculable thousands." The Hebrew wording is similar to Daniel's description of the Ancient of days: "A fiery stream issued and came forth from before him: thousand thousands ministered unto him, and ten thousand times ten thousand stood before him: the judgment was set, and the books were opened" (Daniel 7:10). At the birth of Jesus the angels rejoicing on the Judean hills were called "a multitude of the heavenly host . . ." (Luke 2:13), and at His arrest Jesus said, "Thinkest thou that I cannot now pray to my Father, and he shall presently give me more than twelve legions of angels?" (Matthew 26:53).

John the Revelator testified, "And I beheld, and I heard the voice of many angels round about the throne and the beasts and the elders: and the number of them was ten thousand times ten thousand, and thousands of thousands" (Revelation 5:11). Although he had the more descriptive Greek language at his fingertips, John was no more able to give us a good concept of the numbers of angels that stand before God than David could. It is still an incalculable number. Dr. Franz Delitzsch, in reference to this vast host of angelic beings, says, "It is intended to give a conception of the 'hosts' which Elohim is to set in array against the 'kings of hosts,' i.e., the martial power of the kingdom of the world, for the protection and for the triumph of His own people" (*Commentary on the Old Testament,* volume 5).

If men in the world could only see God in the midst of His thousands of war chariots, their hearts would quake with fear, and if the Church could visualize the tremendous number and power of the angels who have been commissioned by God to serve her, how faith would spring eternally in her midst, but God does not grandstand His Spirit world; He just comfortably moves in the midst of it, totally unseen by the eyes of men.

That God is among them is incontrovertible, for David clearly declares, ". . . even thousands of angels: the Lord is among them" (Psalms 68:17), but who are these myriads of beings called "chariots" and "angels"? The Hebrew word David uses for angels is *shinan*, and this is the only time the word is translated as "angels" in the entire Bible. Apparently the origin of the word is somewhat obscure, for different scholars project different meanings for the word. Some say that it means "vigorous ones" or "happy ones," and certainly it would be difficult to conceive of angels being slothful and unhappy in the presence of God in heaven. Angels do not know the gloom, sorrow, and sadness that characterize so much religious activity here on earth. They know the abiding presence of the Living God, and their countenances are happy and their response is vigorous.

Other students of the Hebrew language feel that this word *shinan* is probably derived from a word which signifies "peaceable" and "quiet," referring to the tranquil state in which the angels live in heaven, always beholding the face of God there. No freeways, or work schedules, or home responsibilities hassle the angels. They do the bidding of God, and God alone, and whatever they do under His commission is done in His power and strength. They cannot identify with our anxieties, for they have lived their eternal existence in the presence of God Almighty who has no occasion for anxiety or for projecting it to others.

I have found still other translators who feel that *shinan* may come from a word which signifies "sharp" and so refers to the angels being the executioners of God's wrath and vengeance on men. Some think it may refer to chariots with scythes or sharp hooks protruding from the wheels intended to mow down infantry soldiers in a time of battle.

A considerable number of the translators feel this word has its origins in a word which signifies "second," suggesting that the angels are next to God, or the chief princes of heaven. Perhaps the very obscurity of the word is good, for we have a very limited comprehension of God's angels anyway. All of these projections are acceptable, for certainly the angels are vigorous, happy ones, peaceable and quiet, and the sharp executioners of God's wrath. That they are second to God presents no problems until the Church arrives in heaven, for there we will be God's Bride, the Lamb's Wife, and that position is generally considered the number-two spot.

But whatever their nature, "The Lord is among them, as in Sinai . . ." (verse 17). The Lord is at the head of them as Governor, and Commander. They are every ready to do His will as the happy, vigorous servants of God. The Lord is among them as He was when He ascended to heaven, or as at Sinai when He gave the Law. They are round about Him, He has them with Him, and He is present with them.

In saying that "The Lord is among them, as in Sinai . . ." (verse 17), David is probably referring to the words of Moses when he was recounting the giving of the law to the second generation. "The Lord came from Sinai," he said, ". . . and he came with ten thousands of saints: from his right hand went a fiery law for them" (Deuteronomy 33:2). It was not merely God and Moses on that mountain; God had brought at least ten thousand of His angels with Him, and they assisted in the giving of the law, as the New Testament affirms. Now David says that just as when God was bringing us into a covenant relationship with Himself, He came with His heavenly host, now that He has brought us into the stability of our inheritance in the Church. He is still among us with His heavenly host. The Reverend A. R. Fausset says, "Sinai and Zion resemble one another in this, that the Lord is on the latter, as he was in the former, encompassed with countless angels" *(Critical and Experimental Commentary,* volume 3). We need to learn to be comfortable in the realization that wherever God is, all of the heavenly hosts are. When God is in His Church, His angels are there with Him. Whether we are aware of them or not, they are working, not at our bidding, but in response to the expressed will of the Father.

Furthermore, wherever God and His holy angels are, true holiness will be demonstrated. Sinai became such an awesome sight of divine holiness that the people could barely stand to look at it. In looking at David's statement that "the Lord is among them, as in Sinai, in the holy place" (Psalms 68:17) Franz Delitzsch said, "We must . . . render it: a Sinai is it in holiness, i.e., it presents a spectacle such as Sinai presented when God by His appearing surrounded it with holiness" (*Commentary on the Old Testament,* volume 5). The Church will never be noted in this world because she has attained heights in education, humanitarianism, social outreach, or numerical growth, but when God and His heavenly hosts show up in the Church, such radiance of holiness emanates as to produce awe, reverence, and terror in the hearts of the beholders. While holiness is not considered popular in or out of the Church, it is the essential nature of God; and where God is, holiness is manifested; and where His holiness is seen, men cannot be unaware that He is there, for much like the lightning, thunder, and earthquakes at Sinai, God's holiness is an unmistakable demonstration of His presence.

God Dwells Among Men

Although it is unmistakably true that God dwells in Zion, His universal Church, and among His angels, it is equally true that God dwells in the local church, or the smaller segments of His Church. David continues his discussion of the dwelling place of God by writing, "Thou hast ascended on high, thou hast led captivity captive; thou hast received gifts for men; yea, for the rebellious also, that the Lord God might dwell among them" (Psalms 68:18).

In speaking of Christ leading captivity captive, some feel that this refers to the saints who were resurrected at the time of Christ's resurrection and went back into Jerusalem to pick up their lives as a testimony of God's power over death (*see* Matthew 27:52–53); others suggest it speaks of the transfer of the righteous dead from Sheol to Paradise. But since neither of these events is keyed to the ascension – each is a part of His resurrection – it is far more likely that the Spirit is speaking of Christ's triumphant stripping of satan as He divested him of all authority and power. Paul describes this in his letter to the church at Colossae in saying, "And having spoiled principalities and powers, he made a shew of them openly, triumphing over them in it" (Colossians 2:15). The Greek word we have translated as "spoiled" is *apekduomai*, which literally means "to divest wholly; to despoil." It is a military term for an action which moviegoers and TV viewers will recognize from western scenes in which an officer of the cavalry is disgracefully stripped of his rank and drummed out of the service. In my recent book *Let Us See Jesus* I deal quite conclusively with this in chapter seven, so I will not repeat myself here. Suffice it to say that at His ascension Jesus took every title, position, authority, and rank from satan and left him stripped, humiliated, and virtually powerless. "All power is given unto me in heaven and in earth," Jesus testified (Matthew 28:18).

Having brought satan and his kingdom back into captivity, Jesus ascended to be reunited with His Father and our Father. Consistent with the concept that ascending potentates sent gifts to their friends and subjects as part of their coronation ceremony, David says that Christ "received gifts for men," that is, the Father gave to the Son gifts that the Son gave to men. This passage is quoted in Ephesians where Paul wrote:

> But unto every one of us is given grace according to the measure of the gift of Christ. Wherefore he saith, When he ascended up on high, he led captivity captive, and *gave gifts* unto men. . . . And he gave some, apostles; and some, prophets; and some, evangelists; and some, pastors and teachers."
>
> EPHESIANS 4:7–8,11 (italics added)

David, from the Old Testament perspective, could see Christ only receiving gifts for men, but from the New Testament point of view we can see that every gift that the Father put into the hands of the Son was distributed to the Church on this earth. In this passage Paul lists three levels of gifts being given by Christ. First, "Unto every one of us is given grace . . ." (verse 7). Oh, how we need it! God's grace – God's love in action – God's unmerited favor – is the difference between life and death for all of us. We dare not receive from God what we deserve – it would be eternal damnation – but we can receive His limitless grace. We will never outgrow our need for divine grace. The gift of grace is the starting point of God's giftings through Christ, and it is an amazingly widespread gift. "For the grace of God that bringeth salvation hath appeared to all men" Paul told Titus (Titus 2:11).

The second level of gifts is the simple statement, ". . . and gave gifts unto men" (Ephesians 4:8). This is not merely a restating of the gifts of grace, for a different Greek word – *domata* – is used, and this word means "sovereign, selective giving." Everybody was given grace, but of those graced individuals God sovereignly selected some and gave them a *domata*. It is quite likely that Paul is referring to those gifts, which he called "pneumatica" in 1 Corinthians 12; we call them the "gifts of the Spirit" or "special abilities imparted by the Spirit." This list of nine special gifts operated by the Spirit in the lives of believers includes three that supernaturally enable us *to know*: word of wisdom, word of knowledge, and the discerning of spirits; three that spiritually enable us *to do:* faith, healings, and miracles; and three that divinely enable us *to speak:* tongues, interpretation of tongues, and prophecy. These gifts have been imparted for the edification, comfort, and encouragement of the Church. Happy is the congregation that both possess and releases them.

The third level of gifts of which Paul speaks is gifted persons that God gives to His Church. God gifts individuals, and then He gives some of those gifted individuals back to His Church. They are listed as the apostle, prophet, evangelist, and pastor/teacher. Since these officeholders have been given by Christ, they are very high gifts to the entire Church and should be received as the gift of God. Repeatedly the Scriptures illustrate that whom God calls, He qualifies with gifts, and then the qualified are given to the Church.

But why this generous giving to the Church? Why such abundant grace? Why such diversity of spiritual gifts? Why have gifted men and women been given to the Church? Is it to build up the Church? That's secondary. Could it be to enable men to develop individual kingdoms? That shouldn't even be considered. The psalmist clearly says that all of the gifts that Christ received from the Father and distributed to the Church are "that the Lord God might dwell among them" (Psalms 68:18). This is the primary purpose of all of God's gifts: to make it possible for us to stand God's presence in an ongoing experience. The gifts of the Spirit have been given to make us comfortable with the presence of God. They enable us to know a little of what He knows; allow us to do a little of what He does; and make it possible for us to communicate a little in spiritual language. This takes away much of the strangeness we used to feel when around the presence of God. They give us enough contact with "supernatural" to make us sufficiently comfortable that we begin to see it as the "norm" in God's world. Nothing God does is supernatural to Him; it is all very natural. Once we get over the extreme sense of awe at the ways, works, and words of God, we can begin to enjoy a comfortable fellowship with God, and that is His ultimate intention for man.

God desires us to enjoy His presence, not merely endure it. He desires a response of joy, not fear, dread, or wonderment. He seeks to so acquaint us with Himself that we desire His presence, and part of this process is to give gifts to men.

God wants to dwell among His people. In the local church where the giftings of God are in operation, you will likely find the presence of God, for God dwells in the Church universal, among His angels, and among those He has so lavishly gifted. And what will be the results of God's presence? We will have blessings beyond our wildest imaginations on a daily basis.

6
God Sustaining

Blessed be the Lord, who daily loadeth us with benefits, even the God of our salvation. Selah. He that is our God is the God of salvation; and unto God the Lord belong the issues from death.

PSALMS 68:19,20

The cry "Let God arise" always carried with it the connotation of God supporting His people. In the wilderness the move was for the benefit of the Hebrews, both for purpose of sanitation and to induce progress toward the Land of Promise. In the subjugation of Canaan God's arising was always for conquest of new territory for His people. In each case, God's presence became the total support system for the people. He led, fed, and fought for His chosen ones, and He undergirded them with divinely chosen leadership and assigned tasks for the people. In supporting His people God sometimes did *for* them, often times did *to* them, and on repeated occasions did *with* them, for sustaining a people does not mean making them weak and dependent by doing everything for them. Often it means teaching them how to do for themselves.

There are times in our pilgimage when God supports us by action beyond ourselves – He does for us – but there are other times when God supports us by action within ourselves – He does a work in us and strengthens us to get involved.

God Loads Us

"Blessed be the Lord," David wrote, "who daily loadeth us . . ." (Psalms 68:19). The words "with benefits" are in italics in the King James Bible indicating that they have been supplied by the translators and do not appear in the original language. The Reverend A. R. Fausset, to whom I have repeatedly referred, informs us that " 'loadeth' may refer to a burden of calamities, not benefits." And *Robert Young's Literal Translation of the Bible* reads, "Blessed is the Lord, day by day He layeth on us." It is possible that Fausset, Delitzsch, Gill, and other commentators are correct in suggesting that it is God who burdens us, or loads us down, even though this thought immediately cuts across the grain of our prior concepts of God as the Source of our blessings.

We are generally taught that at our conversion God unloaded, or unburdened us, freeing us to enjoy a life of liberty in Him. This, of course, is true, but it is only a part of the truth. Just as God liberated the Hebrews from their slavery only to eventually harness them as warriors and ultimately as farmers, so God brings us out of one way of life to "burden," or load us with another. God's salvation was never planned to be a life of inactivity, but of directed activity. We've been delivered from death to enjoy the abundance of life, but life itself is a load – a burdensome load.

Loaded With Controls

God burdens us with *controls*, for hardly has the sinner relaxed from rejoicing over the breaking of satan's yoke from his neck than he hears Jesus saying, "Take my yoke upon you, and learn of me . . ." (Matthew 11:29). Although the power of sinful appetites and passions has been broken, the authority of the Word of God can become a new burden for the young believers, for they soon discover that their liberty is founded on law, and their peace is bounded by precepts.

To the libertines who insist upon the right to do anything they please, the authority of God's Word is something to be avoided, but all freedom is safeguarded by fiat. Where law is withdrawn or ignored, there is lawlessness, not liberty.

The *Chaldaic* translates this verse, "He loadeth us with precept upon precept" (Psalms 68:19). God's Word is not an optional guide to a superspiritual life; it is the obligatory rule book for all born-again Christians. As Corrie ten Boom has so clearly told us, "God's Word contains no suggestions, only commandments." The Bible is a burden God has laid upon us, because without it we would selfdestruct. The sin and misery around us should convince us that man is not capable of guiding his own life; he needs a guide. In spiritual and moral matters man cannot lead – cannot order – he must obey orders. That's why God burdens our lives with His Word. The Word of God "is a lamp unto my feet, and a light unto my path" (Psalms 119:105).

Just as the driver's license that frees us to drive in any of the fifty states of the Union also restricts us with multiple traffic laws, so God's "license" to travel the King's highway carries with it rules, restrictions, and regulations that, while they may seem burdensome at times, safeguard our liberties and rights. Knowing this, the psalmist cried, "Thy word have I hid in mine heart, that I might not sin against thee" (Psalms 119:11). When we embrace, rather than disgrace, the Word of God, we prove that we have learned how to correctly bear the burden that God has imparted to the believer and will discover that what seemed to be a pressing burden turned out to be a progressive blessing, for God's precepts become our protection and the source of our provision.

Loaded With Conviction

God not only loads us down with the burden of controls; He periodically burdens us with *conviction*. If obedience to God's Word were optional, then we would never experience the heavy weight of conviction, but since submission to God's authority is obligatory, there must be a means of enforcement, and conviction is the first stage of that enforcement.

All disobedience to God's precepts is subject to God's punishment, since the Word clearly declares, "The soul that sinneth, it shall die" (Ezekiel 18:4,20), but all divine judgment is tempered with mercy, for "The Lord is . . . not willing that any should perish, but that all should come to repentance" (2 Peter 3:9). God has no pleasure in the punishment of His children, but neither is He an indulgent parent. Rebellion must be removed from His Church, or the disease of sin will destroy the very thing for which Christ died.

Mercifully, the first step in God's judgment of sin in the lives of believers is the conviction of the Holy Spirit. Irrespective of the rationalization the individual may have made, or the extent to which the conscience may have been seared, the Holy Spirit begins a gentle loading with conviction of wrong done. The awareness of having disobeyed God becomes an overriding obsession. Sights, sounds, and smells all seem to trigger the memory circuits, while the duties of the day and the dreams of the night tend to combine in pointing the finger of blame. The joy of living is replaced with the drudgery of existing, and the former song in the spirit is replaced with a sigh in the soul. What was once beauty has now turned to ashes, and the garment of praise is exchanged for the spirit of heaviness. Undergirding every thought is the pervading cry, "I have sinned."

David's passionate night with Bathsheba graphically illustrates this. His acts of adultery and subsequent murder were clear violations of God's commandments, and when the Holy Spirit put His finger of conviction on this sin, David began to fall apart. Day after day he burned in regret, remorse, and fear of divine retribution. During these days when he was burdened to the breaking point with conviction, he wrote the Thirty-second Psalm, which says, "When I kept silence, my bones waxed old through my roaring all the day long. For day and night thy hand was heavy upon me: my moisture is turned into the drought of summer" (Psalms 32:3,4).

But since the purpose of conviction is not to bring us into condemnation but to cause us to confess our sins, once we repent of our rebellion we are released from this burden of conviction. David expressed it this way: "I acknowledged my sin unto thee, and mine iniquity have I not hid. I said, I will confess my transgressions unto the Lord; and thou forgavest the iniquity of my sin" (Psalms 32:5). The burden of conviction may grieve us, but the fruit of conviction – repentance – will bless us, Paul says that "the goodness of God leadeth thee to repentance" (Romans 2:4); so since repentance is the perfect fruit of conviction, the burden of God's conviction is indeed a blessing. It is a good father enforcing the rules of the home in the gentlest manner possible.

Loaded With Concern

Occasionally God "loadeth us" with the burden of *concern*. While indeed "This is my Father's world," as the hymn writer puts it, God has shared the burden of concern with His redeemed children, much as an earthly parent seeks to involve his children with a healthy concern about their person, the house, the others in the home, and even the animal pets kept in the home. The greater the level of maturity the greater is the level of responsibility.

God shares with us the responsibility for our spiritual development and well-being. God, of course, does for us what we are unable to do for ourselves. Failure to understand this principle can lead to spiritual malnutrition and retardation. God supplied an unlimited amount of daily manna for Israel, but each household had to gather and prepare it, or the Hebrews would have starved. God did not force-feed or eliminate the need for eating; He merely made food available.

Similarly, once we grow beyond the baby stage in our spiritual walk with God we are "burdened" with the responsibility of gathering food from the Bible and preparing it in prayer. We are challenged to exercise ourselves unto godliness (see 1 Timothy 4:7); to "pray without ceasing" (1 Thessalonians 5:17), and to forsake not the assembling of ourselves together (see Hebrews 10:25).

Although God has given us apostles, prophets, evangelists, and pastor/teachers to govern, guide, gather, guard, and ground us, the fundamental concern for our spiritual well-being must rest with us. If we are unconcerned we have no right to expect others to be concerned for us. Many years ago, as a pastor, I ceased picking up every prayer burden that was expressed to me. When someone says, "I wish you would pray for me about such and such," I now answer, "Are you praying about it? If not, why should I?" I'm willing to pray *with* people, but not *for* them; that is, I'm willing to share their burden, but I'm unwilling to bear their burden as a surrogate lest I become their substitute for God. All of us need occasional help with a burden, but perhaps the greatest help that can be offered us is instruction in how to bear our own burdens unto the Lord. Self-concern is a burden that God daily "loadeth"upon us.

Beyond a self-concern, God burdens us with a concern for others. "We then that are strong," Paul says, "ought to bear the infirmities of the weak, and not to please ourselves" (Romans 15:1), and later he adds, "Bear ye one another's burdens, and so fulfil the law of Christ" (Galatians 6:2). We Christians have been formed into the "family of God," and as brothers and sisters we have a concern for one another. We are challenged to "confess your faults one to another, and pray one for another, that ye may be healed" (James 5:16). Even godly Paul pled with the saints to continue "praying always with all prayer and supplication in the Spirit . . . *for all saints*; and *for me* . . ." (Ephesians 6:18,19, italics added). In virtually every letter Paul wrote to the churches he assured them that he prayed for them daily, so great was the burden of concern he bore for the saints. How vital it is that believers hold one another up in prayer, for the enemy of our soul is insidious, and his constant attacks wear all of us down occasionally. How very often have I been sustained and strengthened through the earnest prayers of others; I seriously doubt if I could continue in my present level of ministry without them. Although I have chosen to function without formal "prayer partners," or a "prayer-chain," God faithfully burdens some of His choice saints to plead before the throne on my behalf at times of my greatest need.

But none of us has completely borne his burden of concern for other Christians simply by praying for them. Each of us has been challenged to exhort, comfort, warn, encourage, edify, and challenge other family members. We are indeed our brother's keeper. If he sins, we should rebuke him, in love, endeavoring to restore him to fellowship with God. If he errs from the faith, we should teach him the way of God more perfectly. If he undergoes an attack that brings him sorrow, we are responsible to comfort him, and when our brother or sister is discouraged, God expects us to encourage him or her. Even the inactive and sluggish Christian becomes our burden of concern, for the Word says, "let us consider one another to provoke unto love and to good works" (Hebrews 10:24).

No one would deny that this responsibility for our brothers and sisters is a "burden" that God lays on us, but when it is widely borne on a daily basis, it affords mutual protection and personal maturation, for bearing our brother sustains him and strengthens us at the same time.

Sometimes we apply this principle on an individual level without ever considering our responsibility for one another on a corporate level. I was so blessed a short time back to be the guest speaker at a church which was deeply involved in a building program that was costing far more than their architect's estimate. They were earnestly seeking any kind of contribution or loan that they could get. In the Sunday morning service the pastor reported to his congregation that the black congregation in the area they were leaving had a desperate need for a new roof on their church. To my amazement and pleasure this all-white congregation that was experiencing its own financial problems voted unanimously to take money out of its building fund to pay for the reroofing of that black church. They were concerned with the need of a "brother" congregation even though they were not of the same denominational affiliation or cultural background. It hardly needs to be added that when I returned for a conference one year later, this congregation was in its new facility with all financing adequately secured, for they had learned the principle, "Give, and it shall be given unto you . . ." (Luke 6:38).

Concern for others that moves us to prayer or causes us to get involved in helping them is a daily burden sent by God, but it is not always for the "brotherhood." Sometimes God burdens us for the unsaved. He shares a divine compassion for the unconverted that drives us to our knees, causes us to share of our means, and makes enthusiastic witnesses out of us. Men and women seldom get saved until the Church, or individuals in the Church, get concerned over them. Mothers and fathers who pray into the night season for their children will generally see them serving the Lord.

Paul wrote Timothy, "I exhort therefore, that, first of all, supplications, prayers, intercessions, and giving of thanks, be made for all men. . . . For this is good and acceptable in the sight of God our Saviour; Who will have all men to be saved, and to come unto the knowledge of the truth" (1 Timothy 2:1,3,4). Our prayers seem to give God an authority to intervene in the lives of the ungodly and break the power of sin and satan long enough for them to come to a knowledge of God. All sweeping revivals of repentance have come as a response of God to the prayers of interceding saints, for more is wrought through prayer than this world will ever know. When a Christian fastens onto an unbeliever in effectual, fervent prayer, that sinner is already destined for sainthood.

Furthermore, in this same passage where Paul exhorts us to pray "for all men" he specifies that we should pray "for kings, and for all that are in authority; that we may lead a quiet and peaceable life in all godliness and honesty" (1 Timothy 2:2). It may be easier to criticize leadership than to pray for it, but intercession, not faultfinding, is God's burden to His saints for the leadership He has placed over them.

Loaded With a Commission

On repeated occasions the prophets referred to their messages as "the burden of the Lord." They had received both a communication and a commission from God to share that communication, and they called it a "burden." In the sense that they press heavily upon us, all divine commissions become daily burdens; ask the apostles. While the missionary may stand in the convention and declare, "It is a real privilege to serve God in Africa," he would privately admit that it was equally a burdensome task that loses its glamour very quickly; only the awareness of a divine call – the knowledge that the burden came from the Lord – will sustain him on the field in the midst of the pressure. Ministry is work; divine commissions are burdens, for no matter how God may empower the one He commissions, there will always be the burdens of spiritual opposition, human rejection, and personal fear of inadequacies.

Those who enter the full-time ministry out of a misguided zeal or because it appears to be an easy and glamourous life soon discover how heavy the commission can become, and they frequently drop out of service rather quickly. Accepting a divine commission will not be a perpetual vacation, and even preparing to accept the call of God can become a burdensome task, as many of my students at Fountain Gate College will gladly attest.

To be sent of the Lord is indeed an honor, but to rightly represent Him and His holy nature can be a backbreaking burden, very heavy to bear. Even the fundamental commission, ". . . Ye shall be witnesses unto me . . ." (Act 1:8) becomes a daily burden, for it affects our attitudes, expressions, words, relationships with others, and our very way of living. We live no longer unto ourselves, but unto Christ. It is not our will that governs our choices, but God's will. We no longer walk according to the dictates of our flesh, but we now walk in the Spirit.

While God's way of living is far superior to ours, it is in conflict with our carnal natures, and it is consistently at variance with our past training and our present circumstances. To properly live in the light of our commission from God demands a separation from the world that is as burdensome as living in another country surrounded by an alien culture and a foreign language. It can be done, but it is not easy.

Loaded With Circumstances

None of the psalmists could have better understood that God "daily loadeth" us with burdensome circumstances than David, the sweet singer of Israel, for he knew what it was like to run for his life, although he had done nothing to provoke Saul's hatred. He lived in caves and on the open hillsides for years with none but outlaws for his companions. He was acquainted with hunger and cold and knew the terrors of many battlefields. But all of this was God's process of making a king out of a shepherd boy. In an earlier psalm David admitted, ". . . Thou has enlarged me when I was in distress . . ." (Psalms 4:1).

Transformation requires pressure, and God often uses circumstances to exert that pressure upon us. Fanny J. Crosby had to bear the burden of blindness, but from her darkened circumstances came such songs as "Blessed Assurance" and "To God Be the Glory," which have blessed millions of people.

Paul the apostle prepared to go to Asia with the Gospel, but he was hindered by insurmountable circumstances. He responded to a vision and went to Europe instead, for which we Caucasians can give thanks to the Lord.

Life holds many disappointments, but many of them prove to be His appointments. God burdens us with circumstances to effect change in us, to guide us, and to mature us. It often takes the responsibility of marriage to make a man out of a boy, and the coming of a baby quickly makes a woman out of a young lady. Similarly, the burdensome circumstances that God brings into our lives, whether pleasant or unpleasant, enlarge and mature us, making us more valuable to the Body of Christ.

Is going to a job daily a burden or a blessing? Is raising children a burden or a blessing? Is responsibility in the work of the Lord a burden or a blessing? Or could we say that they are a blessing of a burden, for all of these continuing circumstances become the very foundation of life. "Blessed be the Lord, who daily loadeth us . . ." (Psalms 68:19).

God Bears Our Burdens

It is consistent with the teaching of the whole Bible that God who loads us down with burdens is the God who bears us up in the midst of those burdens.

I have not found another Bible translator who agrees with Robert Young, Fausset, Keil-Delitzsch, or Gill in their suggestion that the Hebrew strongly implies that it is God who burdens us down. While I certainly am not scholar enough to disagree with their interpretation of the Hebrew words in this verse, it is significant that most Bible translators have chosen to translate the verse very closely to the King James Bible. The James Moffatt translation reads, "Blessed be the Lord, our saving God, who daily bears the burden of our life," and the Amplified Bible says, "Blessed be the Lord, Who bears our burdens and carries us day by day, even the God who is our salvation!"

That our God is a Burden-Bearer is taught, implied, or illustrated in every division of the Bible. From Israel's deliverance from slavery to Isaiah's cry, "Surely he hath borne our griefs, and carried our sorrows . . ." (Isaiah 53:4), God has revealed himself as ". . . the Lord, who daily beareth our burden" (Psalm 68:19 ASV).

God Bears Our Burdens for Us

While, as I have sought to establish, it is true that God burdens us in this life in order to mature us spiritually and to involve us in ministry in the great family of God, some burdens are of such magnitude as to be unbearable by weak mortals such as we. God knows our frame, for He formed us out of the dust of the earth, and as our Creator He understands our limitations and breaking points, for He has promised that He ". . . will not suffer you to be tempted above that ye are able; but will with the temptation also make a way to escape, that ye may be able to bear it" (1 Corinthians 10:13).

The Load of Sin

The one burden no mortal has ever been able to bear without breaking is the burden of sin. Sin, which promises pleasure, actually produces unbearable pressure. Sin bruises, batters, and battles a person to a bloody pulp. It warps the will, distorts man's basic drives, replaces love with lust, and eventually destroys the body with disease and death. There is no human cure for sin; once it begins it can be neither arrested nor eradicated, and even if the acts of sin are abandoned, the facts of sin's presence produce a gnawing guilt that lasts a lifetime. Man has mastered flight to the moon, but he cannot master the fight in his memories.

Because sin is completely uncontrollable by man, God became man by incarnation, lived as man during His humanity, and died for man at Calvary. "Surely he hath borne our griefs . . ." the prophet declared (Isaiah 53:4), to which the New Testament answers, "Who his own self bare our sins in his own body on the tree, that we, being dead to sins, should live unto righteousness . . ." (1 Peter 2:24). The substitutionary nature of Christ's death and its vicariousness form the theme of the New Testament, which consistently trumpets the message: . . . Christ died for our sins according to the scriptures . . ." (1 Corinthians 15:3). What we could not do, He did for us; what we cannot bear, He bore for us. The guilt that pressed like a two-ton weight has been lifted, leaving us as liberated as an innocent, newborn child. God became man to redeem man from the curse of sin.

The Load of Sorrow

A sideline of sin, and one of its obvious symptoms, is sorrow. Sorrow saps strength and vitality from life and prevents us from enjoying even the simplest pleasures in life. Sorrow numbs our consciousness, dulls our desires, deepens our depression, and challenges our faith. When sorrow reigns, every other emotion in our lives becomes its slave, and it doesn't take long to discover what a severe taskmaster sorrow can be.

The burden of sorrow has been the cause of much alcoholism, drug abuse, and suicide. Attempts to drown out the screams of sorrow underlie much of the immorality and sensuality of our generation, for the pursuit of pleasure always indicates the absence of it in the pursuer's life.

Some sorrow is short-lived, but deep sorrow just doesn't go away; it may be pushed into the subconscious portion of the mind, but a song, a picture, or a fragrance can instantly recall it to the conscious mind. Temporary relief may be obtained, but sorrow remains like a decaying tooth whose pain signals have been drugged into numbness. Only removal of the tooth – or the sorrow – can permanently cure the pain.

The same God who bore the burden of our sins for us bears the sorrows of our lives for us as well. "Surely he hath borne our griefs, and carried our sorrows . . ." the prophet declared (Isaiah 53:4). So convinced was Isaiah that Christ would carry our sorrows that he described Jesus as ". . . a man of sorrows, and acquainted with grief . . ." (Isaiah 53:3).

That God, through Christ, carries our sorrows for us is not to be understood to mean that Christians have total immunity from sorrow. Neither the Bible, history, nor experience in life would support such a postulation. Christians are not immunized against sorrow, they are merely instructed in what to do with their sorrow – bring it to Christ. The psalmist admits that ". . . weeping may endure for a night," but David adds, "but joy cometh in the morning" (Psalms 30:5), and Paul declares, ". . . ye sorrow not, even as others which have no hope" (1 Thessalonians 4:13).

Christ, the "Man of sorrows," enters into our sorrow and bears it for us. We may taste the sorrow, but He takes that sorrow. Many a believer has returned home from the funeral of a loved one with the testimony of David: "Thou hast turned for me my mourning into dancing: thou has put off my sackcloth, and girded me with gladness" (Psalms 30:11). When sorrow is removed, joy returns, for joy is the natural condition of a born-again Christian. "These things have I spoken unto you," Jesus said, "that my joy might remain in you, and that your joy might be full" (John 15:11). Since joy and sorrow are an antithesis, one to the other, Christ bears our sorrows so that we may be filled with His joy. What an exchange!

David did not see this as an exception to the rule, nor did he feel that it would be an occasional experience. He assures us that this is available on a daily basis: "Praise be to the Lord, to God our Saviour, who daily bears our burdens" (Psalms 68:19 NIV).

God Bears Our Burdens With Us

Space does not permit us to catalog all of the burdens of life that God bears *for* us, but be assured that they are manifold, for whatever we cannot do, God does for us. But there is another facet of God's bearing of our burdens wherein He daily bears our burdens *with* us. Sometimes God gives us *release* from burdens; other times He gives us *relief* in the midst of our burden bearing.

God does not rear our children for us, for instance. It is sheer spiritual folly to declare that we are turning our children over to God to raise, for that is a responsibility and burden of parenthood. Still, God will share that burden with us. Many of us parents have been greatly relieved from the frustrations of bringing our children to maturity by spending some time in prayer on a daily basis. Somehow God seems to shoulder much of the weight, and often He gives tips, hints, and guidance to us while we wait in His presence. While He does not bear this burden *for* us, He makes the burden bearable *to* us by sharing the weight *with* us.

The same principle applies to all the burdens we are called upon to bear. God will bear them with us. He lightens the load by becoming a participant, and because He lived as a man among men He knows how to feel with us. "This High Priest of ours understands our weaknesses, since he had the same temptations we do, though he never once gave way to them and sinned" (Hebrews 4:15 TLB). God is neither unknowing nor unfeeling in matters that touch our lives. He lived among us as one of us, and therefore He has personal, firsthand, experiential knowledge about our burdens. He stood where we stand, but He never faltered or failed under any pressure, so now He offers that strength to us.

No wonder, then, that the Jerusalem Bible translates our verse, "Blessed be the Lord day after day, the God who saves us and bears our burdens" (Psalms 68:19 JERUSALEM). He who bears our burdens for and with us daily should be blessed by us daily. He releases us from pressure so that we can respond to Him with praise!

If, however, we choose not to respond to God when the cry "Let God arise" sounds forth, He will not let us go our separate way without severe intervention. Although He will not violate our will, He does graciously bend our will through a process known in the Scriptures as "chastening."

7
God Chastening

**But God shall wound the head of his enemies, and the
hairy scalp of such an one as goeth on still in his trespasses.**
PSALMS 68:21

When God dwells among his people, sustaining them into
security, the cry "Let God arise" is often comparable with a
mother's challenge to the unruly children: "Just wait until
daddy gets home!"

Ideally the family is always at peace with itself and is
consistently obedient to the rules of the home, but
practically there are times of insurrection, disobedience, and
testing of the limits that have been set. That is, when daddy
has to arise.

"Let God arise" is often the cry of the Church when
discipline is needed. Undershepherds can go only so far in
applying discipline, and then, very much like the mother in
the home, their authority is severely challenged. At that
point God arises and sets the Church at rest by judging the
rebels and disciplining the stubborn.

After assuring us of God's sustaining grace and strength in
the midst of life's greatest pressures and problems, David
scores the music of his psalm to strike in *forte* as he declares
that *El*, the "mighty one," is our salvation (*see* Psalms
68:20). God does more than give salvation to His people; He
becomes their salvation. New Testament saints have learned
that salvation is far more than a legal act of God whereby we
are declared rescued from hell; salvation is an ongoing
process that brings us into an intimate relationship with God

such as Adam enjoyed in Eden's garden before the fall. Because our salvation is a continuing process, the dealings of God within our inner natures will also be continuing, including chastisement, in order to bend our wills into conformity with the will of God.

God Chastens His Children

The principle of the chastening of God is almost as old as God's Book itself. Way back in Deuteronomy God had stated, "Thou shalt also consider in thine heart, that, as a man chasteneth his son, so the Lord thy God chasteneth thee" (Deuteronomy 8:5). It is this principle of being chastened of the Lord to which David refers when he says, "But God shall wound the head of his enemies, and the hairy scalp of such an one as goeth on still in his trespasses" (Psalms 68:21). Some translators and commentators seem to feel that this verse shows God "smashing" or "crushing" the head of His enemies in a complete wipeout. However, since the Hebrew word for enemy is *oyabe*, which we saw in chapter one as representing those who are more likely to be seen in the Church than out of it, and since this psalm does not appear to be involved with enemies of God outside the Church (after revealing God warring in verses eleven through fourteen), it is far more probable that David's song commemorates the faithfulness of God our heavenly Father disciplining us into submission to His will, His Word, and His ways.

As further evidence that this verse does not take our thoughts away from the interpersonal relationship of God and His people in order to deal with some outside foe, the psalmist uses the Hebrew word *machats* to describe God's action. "But God shall wound [*machats*] . . . the hairy scalp of such an one as goeth on still in his trespasses" (Psalms 68:21). This word is used fourteen times in the Hebew Bible;

seven times it is translated "wound." and the other times it is translated as "be dipped, pierce, pierce through, smite, smite through, strike through, stroke." Usually where the word is translated as "wound," as here in our psalm, it is balanced with a pledge to heal that wound, such as, ". . . I kill and I make alive; I *wound*, and I heal . . ." (Deuteronomy 32:39, italics added), or "For he maketh sore, and bindeth up: he *woundeth*, and his hands make whole" (Job 5:18, italics added).

Nowhere in the Bible is this word *machats* used for the judgment of God; rather, it seems to speak of a severe chastening that is balanced by subsequent healing and making whole. When judgment is called for, Robert Baker Girdlestone, in his book *Synonyms of the Old Testament*, declares that the Hebrew word *shaphath* is generally used, and that the usual word for "condemnation" is *rasha'*, which in the piel conjugation of this Hebrew verb signifies "to account or deal with the wicked." Reverend Girdlestone lists an additional twelve Hebrew words that are rendered "judge" or "judgment," but *machats* is not among them. It is, therefore, most unlikely that this verse is concerned with the unconverted; it refers specifically to those who have embraced a saving God.

Chastisement Is Not Punishment

When we speak of God chastening His children, we frequently lose sight of the fine line between chastisement and punishment. Punishment is penalty for disobedience, while chastisement seeks to break the spirit of rebellion. Punishment deals with acts; chastisement often deals with attitudes that may, or may not, have become acts. Chastisement is not punishment; it is instruction or training. The Hebrew words for chasten in our Bible are *musar*, which means "instruction or training," and *yasar*, which means "to blind, correct, instruct, reform, teach, or reprove." The Greek word consistently used in our Bible for chastening is *paideuo*, which means "to train up a child, that is, to educate or discipline him." So the real theme of this verse is not pain but pedagogue. It pictures God training His children among whom He dwells and who are sustained and saved by that presence.

Chastisement does not, of itself, forestall punishment, however. While repentance stops the chastening, the inevitable result of our sin may still be realized. A rebelling Christian may in desperation throw himself off the observation tower of the Empire State Building and then during his fall respond to his fear by tearfully repenting before God. And God will mercifully forgive him and restore him to immediate fellowship; but that will not prevent the rest of the downward plunge and its inevitable consequences.

Fortunately, however, by bearing our sins vicariously at Calvary, Christ bore sin's penalty as well, thereby freeing us from living with the consequences of our sin eternally. But although God placed our sins upon Christ Jesus vicariously, He will not chasten Christ in our stead. Each must bear his own chastisement, or else we would never learn much, for even Jesus ". . . learned he obedience by the things which he suffered" (Hebrew 5:8). But Christ was never punished until He took our place on the cross; He was merely chastened, as are all of God's sons. Punishment establishes the chain of retribution, but chastisement reestablishes the lines of authority. Once it is reestablished that God is "boss" and must be obeyed, chastisement ceases. A final contrast between punishment for sin is death, while the chastisement for insurrection is pain.

The Need for Chastening

So far we have seen God related to the enemies, the righteous, the fatherless, the widows, the solitary, the prisoners, the angels, and His Church, but what about those who came into covenant relationship with God but at some point in His leadership have rebelled? What about the self-willed? the stubborn? the sassy saint? There are always those who are in the family but who are unsubmissive to the Father. They are residents of the home but rebellious against the restrictions and rules. Often they actually do what is right, but they despise doing it. Their acts and their attitudes do not harmonize. What will be God's relationship to them?

"Fools because of their transgression, and because of their iniquities, are afflicted" (Psalms 107:17), the psalmist declares. God summarily deals with rebellion, stubbornness, deceit, and unsubmissiveness with chastisement. He teaches us by chastening us. There is a great deal of learning to be found in the application of the board of education to the seat of learning. Someone has rightly said that a pat on the back is a marvelous aid to learning if it is administered often enough, hard enough, and low enough. God is gloriously capable of doing this to us and for us.

Nevertheless, God is not too quick to spank. He yearns that we be precept directed rather than pain motivated. Even after we have violated the known will of God, He gives us space, in which to repent. In the letter to the church at Thyatira, God speaks of Jezebel, a self-proclaimed prophetess, who seduced His servants into fornication and idolatry, and says, ". . . I gave her space to repent of her fornication; and she repented not" (Revelation 2:21). Even in the light of open violation of God's laws of purity, and in the face of the fact that she was teaching this impurity to others, all in the name of God, there was no immediate action. God gave her space to repent. Surely He does the same for us in our periods of transgression.

Tragically, we are tempted to believe that this "space to repent" is tantamount to God's approval of our behaviour. Expecting immediate judgment, but instead receiving evi dence of the divine presence, we sometimes fail to realize that God is seeking to draw us to Himself and away from the sin by loving us in a most overt manner. If we ever need the presence of God, it is when we have an open door to the devil, and whenever we are in open violation to the known will of God we are a wide-open channel to satan. Our sin makes us legally subject to the demonic realm, but God's presence protects and perserves us anyway.

Nonetheless, we dare not misinterpret this presence of God as divine approval of our misbehaviour. In the counseling chambers I have repeatedly heard sinning saints plead the manifest presence of Christ in their lives as evidence that God was allowing them a "special dispensation of grace" and was exempting them from the clear commands of the Word of God. But if God would not wink at sin when it was in His Son, Jesus, at Calvary, it is most unlikely that He will wink at our sin.

Quite frankly, we'll never get by with anything for which the Lord has convicted us, for once God puts His finger on a sin He never removes it. He doesn't stop dealing with us, but He will give us space to repent. The amount of space He will give us varies according to our relationship with Him. Some seem to get years in which to make things right, while others have but a few days to repent. Apparently the more intimate the relationship – the more of us that God owns – the less time we get to set things right in the relationship, much as we expect quick response from our children but allow months for a neighbor to correct his inappropriate behaviour toward us.

The need for chastisement – the reason for it – is that we go on still in our trespass; ". . . for they refuse to leave their guilty, stubborn ways," the Living Bible puts it (Psalms 68:21). We have been warned and wooed; now we will get walloped!

In the *Keil-Delitzsch on the Old Testament*, Dr. Franz Delitzsch says, "The hair-covered scalp is mentioned as a token of arrogant strength, and unhumbled and impenitent pride . . . and directly signifies to strut along, give one's self airs" (volume 5). Pride, arrogance, stubbornness, and self-centeredness will set us up for divine chastisement. God will correct, reform, reprove, and instruct us by chastening us until we change.

The Manner of Chastening

It is appropriate that David declares that God's original dealings are with the mind, for that is where rebellion starts. All arrogance, stubbornness, self-centeredness, rebellion, and pride have their origins in the mind, so God comes against the mind, or the head, which holds the position of authority in our life. God offers to deliberate with us, to talk things over with us, to make a rational approach, or to allow us to lay our intellect alongside His and see which argument is the most germane.

Isaiah spoke of this willingness of God to reason with us when he wrote, "Come now, and let us reason together, saith the Lord: though your sins be as scarlet, they shall be as white as snow; though they be red like crimson, they shall be as wool" (Isaiah 1:18). While this verse has been the text for many an evangelistic sermon, to me it seems a most unlikely picture of steps in redemption, for God does not change red sins into white ones. Instead, He removes sin completely; He cleanses us from all sin! Nowhere else in the Bible will we find a verse that speaks of God merely changing the color of our sins. No, far from picturing the progression out of sin, it graphically illustrates the downward progression of sin in the life of an insurrecting saint.

In Leviticus God gave the priests the laws and tokens whereby a priest was to be guided in discerning leprosy. It is notable that the first thing the priest looked for was a bright, or red, spot on the skin. The presence of such a red spot was sufficient suspicion of leprosy that the person was shut up for seven days and then reexamined. If the red spot turned to white, the person was declared to have the plague of leprosy and was put outside the camp, completely ostracized from all society. He was declared an incurable leper (*see* Leviticus 13).

Actually, Isaiah was saying something like this, "Come now, let us reason together, saith the Lord: although your sins right now are no more than a red spot, their ultimate progression is to become as white as snow. You'll be leprous from head to foot, separated from society, separated from all that is holy, and condemned in your sin." The ultimate end of small sin is big corruption, for it never stays red; it always progresses to white.

Remember that at the burning bush when Moses trembled at the commission God was giving him and doubted if Pharaoh would ever believe that he had actually been sent of God, God told Moses, "Put now thine hand into thy bosom. And he put his hand into his bosom; and when he took it out, behold, his hand was *leprous as snow*" (Exodus 4:6 italics added). Later, when Miriam insurrected against the authority of Moses, God dealt with her very rapidly, ". . . and, behold, Miriam became *leprous, white as snow:* and Aaron looked upon Miriam, and, behold, she was leprous" (Numbers 12:10, italics added). Thus consistently through the Scriptures the final end of leprosy was whiteness, and the final end of sin is absolute putrefaction through the whole of our system. God is simply warning us that the progression of sin is always downward – from bad to worse. There is no such thing as containing a little sin; it will break out. What starts small gets big; what's only a little red spot becomes white.

God first appeals to the head – the mind – because if we can be reasoned out of our sin we need not be rebuked in it. God first communicates; then He chastens. He reasons; then He reprimands. If we heed, He will not hit. If we continue, He will chasten.

The Chastenings of God Are Progressively Severe

Our sin is not the only thing that progresses from little to big; God's chastisements progress from slight to severe. He comes against our rebellion with discipline that matches our resistance. The prophet Hosea speaks of this in most graphic terms when addressing the sinning people and priests of Israel and Judah. ". . . therefore I will pour out my wrath upon them like water," he says (Hosea 5:10). Since water is a type of the Holy Spirit, the first impression in reading this is of God blessing these sinning ones; but the coming of the Spirit is not always in gentleness. "When he is come," Jesus said, "he will reprove the world of sin, and or righteousness, and of judgment" (John 16:8). The water of the Spirit may be gentle rain (*see* Joel 2:23), or it may be a cascading river that undermines the very foundations of what we are doing in our rebellion, or it may be "floods upon the dry ground" (Isaiah 44:3) uprooting, inundating, and devastating everything in our lives. I've watched the work of the Spirit during periods that we call "revival." As the Spirit of the Lord moved upon His Church, it built some people, birthed others, and totally devastated a few. If they would not be chastened, God's Spirit seemed to strip them the way a flood strips a housing development. Only concrete foundations remain.

The second step in God's chastisement is "Therefore will I be unto Ephraim as a moth . . ." (Hosea 5:12). If we will not respond to God's dealings as the water, God begins His dealings as the moth, working secretely upon the treasures in our inner closet. We don't even know it is happening until we pull the coat or sweater out to wear it and find it full of holes. Much like Samson of old, we "wist not that the Lord was departed . . ." (Judges 16:20) until it is gone and we try to demonstrate it. God prefers to chasten His children privately, but if we will not heed Him, He will do it publicly.

In his delineation of the onward progression of God's discipline, Hosea says, "Therefore will I be . . . to the house of Judah as rottenness" (Hosea 5:12). Again it is inner and quiet, but all we have held precious and dear is turning to rottenness, and its stench is easily discernible to others. Just because God doesn't immediately hit us over the head doesn't mean He isn't working with us. It may be as the gentle undermining of water, the secret eating of the moth, or the unseen rotting inwardly, but God is working against us in the inner recesses of our lives.

But if we won't respond to these dealings, God has more. "I will be unto Ephram as a lion . . ." (Hosea 5:14). The Hebrew word we have translated as "lion" here is *shachl*, which comes from a root that means "to roar." It pictures the older lion roaring at the trembling prey. God will roar, or will cause His Word to roar at us. He can cause all life to roar His threats at us, and the roar of the lion, as the roar of God, is fearsome, terrorizing, immobilizing, and anxiety producing, for the lion's roar signals death and destruction. It is either flee or feed the lion – with Me!

Nonetheless, if we will not submit to the roar of God, God instructs Hosea to say, "I will be . . . as a young lion to the house of Judah . . ." (Hosea 5:14). Interestingly, Hosea uses a different Hebrew word for "lion" here in using *kephiyr*, which signifies "a young lion." It will no longer be the threatening roar of the old lion; it is pursuit time. The young lion is the fighter, the predator, and the conqueror. He has the speed and strength to prevail over his quarry. This lion is not the devil; it is God Himself who is declared to be "the lion of the tribe of Judah" (Revelation 5:5). Satan is not a lion; he can only imitate the roar of a lion. If gentleness and fear cannot remove us from our wayward route, then God will wound and tear us as a lion does its prey. ". . . I, even I, will tear and go away; I will take away, and none shall rescue him" (Hosea 5:14). Young lions often kill and leave the game for other animals to clean the carcass. We will not be forsaken by God until he has torn us completely. "None shall rescue him," Hosea warns. Once the "young lion" does his work, it is too late to run to the world for solace, or to the Church for help; God will not let them bind us up, For God is trying to chasten us back to obedience and submission to divine authority.

In this final step of His chastisement God says, "I will go and return to my place, till they acknowledge their offence, and seek my face: in their affliction they will seek me early" (Hosea 5:15). It is tragic that we force God to deal so harshly with us before we will seek His face, but when God blesses us we sometimes become proud. It is when He banishes us as bleeding corpses that we seek His face. We sometimes force God to take our jobs away from us, or to bring sickness into our homes, rottenness into our bodies, afflictions into our spirits, or car accidents or financial reverses into our lives before we will seek Him.

It is sheer foolishness to make God use such harsh, drastic, and penalizing means of discipline, for He first came as gentle water, and then with the inner workings of a moth and rottenness. It is our refusal to heed the gentle dealings that forces God to use the severe dealings of the lion in pouncing, wounding, lacerating, and finally departing from us until in our weak, wounded condition we begin to seek God with our whole heart.

But no matter how severely God must deal with us to get us to return to seeking Him and His presence, there is nothing on earth that is completely irreparable while we can repent and turn unto the Lord; but it must be done with the whole heart! The same Lord that tears, heals; and He who smites, binds up. This is consistent with every use of the Hebrew word *machats* when it is translated "wound." "Come, and let us return unto the Lord," the prophet pleads, "for he hath torn, and he will heal us; he hath smitten, and he will bind us up" (Hosea 6:1). The purpose of the smiting is to get us to return, and until we return we will lay in the dust and bleed our spiritual life onto the ground. If, however, we do turn to God with our whole heart, "then shall we know, if we follow on to know the Lord: his going forth is prepared as the morning . . ." (Hosea 6:3). God chastens us that we would follow on to know the Lord. We are diciplined to discover that God is not merely "boss"; He is everything that is being revealed in this Sixty-eighth Psalm. He gets our attention, and then He instructs us!

We are aware, of course, that God may employ varied tools in His chastisements. Hosea was not exhausting God's methods in suggesting four ways God comes against a stubborn saint. It is God's nature to bring us back into harmony with Himself, His Word, and His Church, but He has so many different ways of doing this. For instance, in dealing with Israel God frequently used her enemies to chasten her back into fellowship with God. When Israel as a nation walked away from God, He merely turned the surrounding enemies against her and sent her into captivity for a season. Some have wondered why it was that upon Israel's entrance into the Promised Land, God did not destroy all of the enemies, but when we see them being used as a whip in the hand of the Heavenly Father to chasten Israel again and again, we understand better. If God were to throw the devil into the Lake of Fire today, the Church would probably never be purified in God's presence, for God still uses the enemy as a tool of chastisement for our own good.

In the case of Nebuchadnezzar, Hezekiah, and others, God used sickness as His chastening tool to bring them to submission to the divine will. In spite of some rather simplistic theology taught today, God does touch our physical bodies in order to chasten us. Pain is a powerful persuader, and God uses it when words fail to change our behaviour patterns.

Sometimes God even uses natural calamities as a chastening tool. Jonah is a good example of this. He endured the catastrophe of a storm, a trip in the whale, fighting his way through a fish's vomit, and even the loss of the protective vine. All of these physical circumstances were used of God to chasten Jonah back into the divine will. Natural calamities are potential tools of God to awaken people to God's claims upon them. Recently I had lunch with a precious saint who told me how God allowed her beautiful new house to be struck by lightning and be completely destroyed by fire as a tool to bring the family back to God. "The results have become so precious," she told me, "that I would welcome another bolt of lightning on our new house if that is what it would take to bring us back to the fellowship with God we have found as a result of the first lightning strike." I assured her that since the family was walking in an intimate relationship with God at this time, they needed no further chastening. God's chastisement had produced its "peaceable fruit of righteousness."

Of course, not all negative circumstances are the dealings of God. Sometimes we create our own reverses. Sometimes we are but the victims of overall circumstances, and other times God is dealing with a whole area and His children merely suffer the "fallout" of that dealing. But we should always take a look at the potential of God's hand being behind all calamities in our lives. If we've been ignoring the water, the moth, the rottenness, and the roaring lion, we can probably accept that this "rending and tearing" is from the "lion of the tribe of Judah," for God will get our attention one way or another.

The Mercy of Chastening

David said, "God shall wound . . . the hairy scalp of such an one as goeth on still in his trespass" (Psalms 68:21). How merciful God is to wound us where the scars will not show. He does not disfigure us – He wounds us. His goal is not to make us the object of the mockery of others; He merely wants us to return to the authority of God in our lives, so He does not strike us across the face He wounds us in the scalp. We are not marked, like Cain, so that all will know we have the judgment of God on our lives. Some local churches have a predisposition to place a "Cain" mark upon the errant members, but God doesn't. When God wounds, we have a tender spot that is known only to God and to us. God hides the scars in our hairy scalp.

There are at least three reasons that God wounds us. The first is that it saves us from destruction. Paul said, "But when we are judged, we are chastened of the Lord, that we should not be condemned with the world" (1 Corinthians 11:32). Through chastisement the Christian is spared condemnation, for "There is therefore now no condemnation to them which are in Christ Jesus . . ." (Romans 8:1). However, if we refuse to submit to the chastisement of God, we will undoubtedly come into the condemnation of the world, for if we refuse to submit to God, we cannot remain in Christ Jesus. God disciplines us that we might escape damnation.

A second reason God chastens us is that it is an evidence of His love. "As many as I love, I rebuke and chasten: be zealous therefore, and repent" (Revelation 3:19). God's chastening is not proof of His disapproval; it is proof of His love, for God never disapproves of us but rather of our arrogant, unsubmitted behaviour. God loves us enough to chasten us back into proper behaviour patterns.

Many years ago when my youngest daughter was in mid-teens, there was an area of her behaviour that she would not bring into conformity to the rules of the home. It seemed that no form of chastening we had used on previous occasions would change her behaviour, so I threatened to take my belt to her if she repeated that conduct. She did – and I did. Lying on my bed crying in deep sobs after spanking her thoroughly, I became aware that she was repeatedly dialing out on the telephone. I picked up the extension phone in our bedroom, to overhear her phoning one after another of the teens in our church to share this brief message: "My dad just gave me the most severe whipping of my life. Boy, how he loves me!"

She had pushed and pushed past the line established by the authority of our home, and she felt very loved and secure in having that authority say, "Back up," even if the process inflicted pain on her. Her attitude was "He is concerned enough about me to make me obey. He loves me." She was able to accept severe chastisement as an evidence of love rather than as an act of frustration or judgment, and so should we.

The third reason that God chastens us is to make us partakers of His holiness. In speaking of earthly fathers chastening us, the Word says "For they verily for a few days chastened us after their own pleasure; but he for our profit, that we might be partakers of his holines (Hebrews 12:10). God does not merely chasten us so we will automatically do what He says, but so that we can progressively become partakers of His holiness. He wants to make us to be holy, and that means that He must come against all that is unholy with whatever measures are necessary. He yearns to make us become like Himself. He desires that we be His children in nature as well as in name, and it takes chastening to change us; so He will discipline our deportment until our behaviour becomes a credit to our Saviour.

Chastisement Offers Us Security

This same passage in Hebrews assures us that ". . . whom the Lord loveth he chasteneth, and scourgeth every son whom he receiveth. If ye endure chastening, God dealeth with you as with sons . . ." (Hebrews 12:6,7). Surely we have learned by now that we spank only our own children. We may correct other children verbally, but the chastening authority is vested in their parents. If, then, God chastens us, it is proof positive that we are indeed His children, for, again, God spanks only His own children. The chastening is not disavowal but acceptance of His parental role in our lives.

Furthermore, God's chastisement is both protection and security for us. David said, ". . . thy rod and thy staff they comfort me" (Psalms 23:4). The shepherd's rod was a throwing instrument that was sometimes hurled at a predatory animal and often thrown at the wandering sheep to knock it down, while the staff was frequently used to drag the sheep back to the flock. God sets boundaries and then enforces them, even if He must knock us down and then drag us back, for He protects us not only from the enemies but from ourselves. Nothing can stop the spirit of wanderlust faster than being on the receiving end of God's rod.

This assurance of God's faithfulness in chastening us, even if He uses the rod and staff, takes the dread and fear out of missing the will of God. If we miss God's will through ignorance, He will reinstruct us. If we miss God's will through stubbornness, He will break us, for God will chasten His children back into His perfect will. How the enemy likes to terrorize the children of God with the fear of missing the will of God. We need not fear being out of God's will. God will both show us the way that we should go and will, if necessary, fence us in on all sides, making missing the will of God obvious and very painful.

Christians should not fear the chastening rod of their loving God; we should favor it. Just as the most miserable child in the home is the one who is getting by in disobeying the rules of the home, so the most miserable saint in God's household is the one who is allowed to flaunt his disregard for God's rules and authority. God loves us too much to allow us to live in such misery. We need to know that if we violate God's will, we won't be snatched from grace, we won't miss the will of God, we won't lose the favor of the

Father, or won't even be left to our own ways; we will merely experience repeated chastenings from the hand of God. This chastisement is instruction, training, reformation, and correction. God readjusts our behaviour, reforms our will, and retunes our attitudes. Just as David affirms that "the steps of a good man are ordered by the Lord . . ." (Psalms 37:23), so God orders our steps to make good persons out of us, and part of that ordering is applied chastisement.

Chastisement is not coercion that violates our will; it is a means of keeping us within the boundaries of the covenant we made with God at our own personal Sinai. It is, if you please, an enforcement of the code we had previously entered into with God. Chastisement is not God's anger; it is a stimulus that compels obedience to accepted standards. This chastening of His children is in such stark contrast to the way God deals with His enemies when He chooses to avenge His people. You should see God avenging!

8
God Avenging

The Lord said, I will bring again from Bashan, I will bring my people again from the depths of the sea: That thy foot may be dipped in the blood of thine enemies, and the tongue of they dogs in the same.

PSALMS 68:22–23

During the days of Moses the proclamation "Let God arise" was a signal to nomadic Israel that a change in locale was in the offing – God was moving on. During Joshua's conquest of the land it became a battle cry which challenged Israel's army to conquest, but during the period of the judges it became the desperate cry of an oppressed people pleading with Jehovah for deliverance from trouble. Assured that God dwelt among them, they expected divine intervention when needed. "Let God arise" to avenge us of our enemies!

The Promise of Vengeance

Both inside and outside the Church far too many of us seem to think that being a Christian means lying down and letting everybody walk over us while we smile sweetly and say, "That's all right; I'm a servant of God." But does being a Christian mean that a wife must suffer physical and emotional abuse at the hands of her unconverted husband? Does embracing Christ as our Saviour mean that our missionaries can be murdered and martyred with impunity? Does meekness mean weakness? Where is the righteous Judge of the earth who enforces equity and truth?

Occasionally Christians take it into their own hands to enforce equality and personal rights, but they usually find that they cannot handle the anger, resentment, and desire for recompense. Their lust for vengeance becomes consuming as they crave "an eye for an eye," and too often they destroy themselves more than they execute vengeance upon the enemy. Knowing that we are too weak to handle this matter of vengeance, God chose to maintain the right to execute the vengeance of His people. The Old Testament law affirms. "To me belongeth vengeance, and recompence; their foot shall slide in due time: for the day of their calamity is at hand, and the things that shall come upon them make haste" (Deuteronomy 32:35). Paul picked up this theme in his letter to the saints at Rome and penned, "Dearly beloved, avenge not yourselves, but rather give place unto wrath; for it is written, Vengeance is mine; I will repay, saith the Lord" (Romans 12:19). So vengeance does not belong to us, but it will be extracted for us by the Lord.

Sometimes it seems that God is mighty slow in executing vengeance upon our enemies. "O Lord God, to whom vengeance belongeth; O God, to whom vengeance belongeth, shew thyself," the psalmist cried (Psalms 94:1), to which the New Testament answers, "For we know him that hath said, Vengeance belongeth unto me, I will recompense, saith the Lord. And again, The Lord shall judge his people" (Hebrews 10:30). We know the *who* vengeance and we are affirmatively promised that He will judge His people, and the implication of the verse is that His people will win their case.

We have an avenging God who rises up and inflicts suffering in requital for wrong done to His children, but He chooses the what and where of that vengeance. Quite often God avenges things that we would not have avenged, while ignoring the things we want avenged most, for often when we want vengeance we are actually seeking self-justification, but God totally disassociates His vengeance from our pride levels and concerns Himself with our safety. God's vindictiveness is never merely to placate His anger; it is always for the betterment of His Church. God comes against the enemy when that enemy is impeding the progress of the Church.

The Pattern of Vengeance As Seen in the Sea

". . . I will bring my people again from the depths of the sea" David wrote (Psalms 68:22). If God is going to bring His people "again," then He must have brought them at least once before. When we remember that David was singing this ode to his fellow countrymen while dancing before the Ark upon its return to Jerusalem, it becomes obvious that the only sea experience that would be well-known to them was the parting of the Red Sea under the rod of Moses (*see* Exodus 14:13–31). The family of Jacob, who left Canaan due to famine conditions, entered Egypt as the guests of Pharaoh because of Joseph. Their four hundred years' residence there can be summarized in saying that they began in favour, fell into disfavour, and ended up in abject salvery. Of course they did not lose their freedom in one quick fell swoop; it eroded from them little by little, just as satan does not attempt to bring us into bondage in one great frontal assault but systematically restricts one freedom after another until we find ourselves servants doing his will even in spiritual matters. Freedom is rarely captured; it is usually surrendered.

Mercifully, God raised up a deliverer in the person of Moses; and through a lengthy series of plagues and judgements upon Egypt and her inhabitants, Pharaoh finally released the Hebrews to go into the wilderness to worship their God Jehovah; but it was very definitely against his better judgement, for the entire economy of Egypt was based upon slavery. Moses' demand for the release of the slaves was tantamount to an unknown zealot's approaching our president with a demand that all of America's automobiles be buried in the Atlantic Ocean and all electrical power turned off, for this would not inconvenience America any more than the loss of the Hebrew slaves paralyzed Egypt.

Amidst the agony of the death of Egypt's firstborn sons, Pharaoh thrust the Hebrews out of the land, but when the extent of the collapse of Egypt's economy began to manifest itself, Pharaoh's counselors urged him to pursue the Hebrews with the army and recapture them for service to the land. Egypt's crack charioteers had no difficulty overtaking the slaves, who had fled on foot, and they soon had them trapped at the Red Sea. So conditioned were the Hebrews to the whiplashes of their former taskmasters that when they saw Egypt's armed might in pursuit they cried out against Moses, ". . . it had been better for us to serve the Egyptians, than that we should die in the wilderness," to which Moses responded "Fear ye not, stand still, and see the salvation of the Lord, which he will shew to you today; for the Egyptians whom ye have seen today, ye shall see them again no more for ever. The Lord shall fight for you, and ye shall hold your peace" (Exodus 14:12–14). In the midst of this dialogue ". . . the Lord said unto Moses . . . speak unto the children of Israel, that they go forward; But lift thou up they rod, and stretch out thine hand over the sea, and divide it: and the children of Israel shall go on dry ground through the midst of the sea" (Exodus 14:15,16).

Moses was in a predicament. He had mountains to the right of him, marshes to the left of him, a sea in front of him, a pursuing army division behind him, a fearful, murmuring people with him; and God's order to him was "Go forward." When Moses obediently stretched forth his rod, God performed a four-fold miracle. First, God sent a strong east wind all night long to divide the sea. Obviously God could have done it with a word, but by parting the waters a little at a time He built faith in the murmuring congregation. God has a way of reducing the fervor of our fears with the wind of

His Spirit! Furthermore, God does things progressively because the more He does the less we fear, and the less we fear the more we can believe. The speed with which God works is keyed more to the faith response within us than to the power within God. He created the world with His word, but in human affairs He does things gradually so as to build faith within us rather than destroy it through fear.

The second phase of the miracle was to move the cloud from in front of Israel to behind her, becoming darkness to the enemy but light to the saints. Whenever the glory of God comes into worship service, it is only the saints who can see it as light; those who are rebelling against God see the whole visitation as dark, foolish nonsense that blinds them to the workings of God.

God withstood Israel's enemy until sufficient faith was available for this multitude to walk through the Red Sea, at which time they discovered the third aspect of God's miraculous provision. They walked through the sea on ". . . dry ground: and the waters were a wall unto them on their right hand, and on their left" (Exodus 14:22). No mud bogged them down, and there was no chance for the enemy to come against them on the right or left flanks. They were really "shut in with God" in the midst of the sea. How much time was required to get them through the sea is not told, but if, as Adam Clarke suggests, there were 4.5 million people who came out of Egypt bringing the flocks and herds of the land with them, it must have taken quite some time for passage; yet the seabed remained firm, and the walls of water did not crumble during this whole time.

When Egypt's mighty men of war pursued the last stragglers from Israel's camp, the fourth step in the miracle occurred. The pathway through the sea which should have been made all the more solid by the passage of so many feet suddenly became quagmire, bogging both the horses and the chariots into immobility, and then the walls of water came tumbling down upon them, drowning the entire army; the

Bible affirms that ". . . there remained not so much as one of them" (Exodus 14:28).

The Benefits of This Vengeance

In one catastrophic stroke God accomplished three things. First, He revealed His power to His people early in their walk with Him. Throughout the entire Old Testament this miracle is given as a measurement of God's divine power, just as the resurrection of Jesus Christ from the dead becomes the measurement of God's power in the New Testament. After such a magnificent miracle, Israel should never again have doubted God's power.

Second, God removed a long-standing enemy from the lives of an entire generation. The enemy did not flee from before them; he drowned in the sea behind them, and their bodies washed up on the wilderness side of that sea, making it possible for Israel to take their armor in order to equip themselves for future warfare.

Third, beyond displaying His power and destroying their enemy, God also avenged Himself and His people for 400 years of cruel slavery at the hands of the Egyptians. "Rejoice," Moses wrote, ". . . for he will avenge the blood of his servants, and will render vengeance to his adversaries, and will be merciful unto his land, and to his people" (Deuteronomy 32:43).

Unquestionably generations of Hebrews had lived and died crying out to God for vengeance, but when God's time came, the vengeance was total and complete. In her exodus Israel had spoiled the Egyptians in collecting 400 years' back wages, but that was compensation, not vengeance. God extraced an "eye for eye, tooth for tooth, hand for hand, foot for foot, burning for burning, wound for wound, stripe for stripe" (Exodus 21:24,25), as He later stipulated in His law.

It is likely that God would have let Egypt get by with mere compensation if she had willingly let God's people go, but any time an enemy withstands God's people, refusing to let them have their liberty, God moves in serious vengeance against that enemy. When God commands a power or person to "let my people go, that they may serve me" (Exodus 9:1), it is asking for divine vengeance to refuse, for once God sets out to liberate His people there is no power on earth or in hell that can hinder Him. The enemy can either release us willingly or face destructive vengeance from God, whether that enemy is the world, the flesh, the devil, or religion. None has ever been able to keep captive those whom God has declared should be set free. Jesus said, "If the Son therefore shall make you free, ye shall be free indeed" (John 8:36). What can an enemy say that will countermand the clear affirmation of God Himself?

The Pattern of Vengeance Illustrated by Bashan

"The Lord said, I will bring again from Bashan . . ." (Psalms 68:22). In chapter four we saw that Bashan was a type of world power that set itself against Zion, God's Church. But here David is not dealing in typology so much as he is recounting history in order to set a precedent for God's vengeance. The incident to which he refers is recorded in the third chapter of Deuteronomy where Moses, in leading the second generation of Israelites toward the borders of the Promised Land, is withstood by Og, the king of Bashan. "So the Lord our God delivered into our hands Og also, the king of Bashan, and all his people: and we smote him until none was left to him remaining" (Deuteronomy 3:3). This area, here called Bashan, is also called "the land of Og" and "the land of the giants."

There are amazing parallels in these two stories. Moses records that this battle against King Og was in the fortieth year and the eleventh month of the travels of the children of Israel, putting this incident within one month of their entry into Canaan, for they entered on the forty-first year following their exodus from Egypt. The story of the sea is at the beginning of the wilderness wandering, while the story of the Ogites is at the end. Both of them are concerned with an armed band of trained soldiers who are determined to prohibit something. The Egyptians made up their minds that they would prohibit the Hebrews from *going out* from their land, while the Bashanites had determined to prohibit the Israelites from *coming into* the land.

The first thrust of the miracle of the Red Sea was to reveal God's mighty power to a great mass of freed slaves. The first thrust of the miracle of the destruction of the Bashanites was equally a manifestation of God's power to a second generation, who had spent forty years wandering in the wilderness because of the report brought by ten of their spies that the land was filled with mammoth giants. No matter how tall those giants had been described as being when the spies gave their fearful report to that first generation, it is to be supposed that the telling and retelling of the story over forty years had greatly exaggerated their size. Now on the eve of their entrance into the land that their parents had refused to enter, God mercifully allows the second generation to be confronted by the last remaining giant, King Og, whose iron bed was about six feet wide and fourteen feet long (*see* Deuteronomy 3:11). Rather than letting them be as grasshoppers in their sight, as the spies had reported, God's presence and leadership caused this second generation of Israelites to be "more than conquerors."

During the forty years while the first generation of unbelieving Israelites was dying off, the giants had also perished. Og was the only giant that the second generation would ever see, for although the book of Joshua speaks twice of giants – once of "the valley of the giants," and once of "the land of the giants – they never found a giant in the land of God's promise. Similarly, in a most amazing way, when we visualize the enemy as so large that our fear cannot receive God's faith, God cuts the enemy down to a size smaller than our faith in God so that we will wholly follow God. When our devil is too big and our God is too small, God reduces the devil down in our sight so that we will fear only the Lord our God.

Many generations later, God let five giants come onto the scene so that still another generation could feel what it was like to slay giants; David slew Goliath, and his mighty men later slew the four brothers. God reinforced the truth that the enemy cannot produce giants bigger than God's ability to kill them off for or with us.

Each generation of believers needs a fresh demonstration of the power of God, whether it be the parting of the sea or the slaying of a giant, for the continuation of what was a miracle for generation number one is merely the accepted norm for the second generation. Freedom from slavery and daily manna ceased to be demonstrations of the power of God to the second geration, who had known nothing else all of their lives, so God demonstrated Himself to them in a different fashion by destroying King Og, the giant.

But it is equally true that each generation needs complete victory over the enemy. In the story of the battle with the Bashanites we are assured that God removed this enemy as surely as the closing of the Red Sea had removed the Egyptians from the first generation, but this time the entire race of the Bashanites was destroyed, in contrast to the annihilation of merely the army of Egypt. This was one enemy that they would not have to battle repeatedly, for never again in the Word of God do we read of an Ogite or a Bashanite after this third chapter of Deuteronomy, and yet there is no record of the death of one Hebrew soldier in the slaughter of this entire nation. God fought this battle; it was not war between two nations but was God's vengeance upon a single nation, Bashan. The Hebrews were merely God's tool.

The first generation saw God take vengeance on Egypt for trying to prohibit their going out of captivity, while the second generation saw God devastate an entire nation with vengeance because they tried to hinder this people from going into the Land of Promise. For forty years Israel wandered because of the paralyzing fear the giants of the land of Bashan had produced, and when King Og withstood the second generation, God said, "That's enough!"

How the Church of Jesus Christ needs to be reminded that whatever seeks to restrict her from coming out of bondage or to prohibit her from coming into her inheritance will experience the inexhaustible vengeance of God. When God says, "Come out," none can keep us in, and when God says, "Enter in," none can keep us out. No man, no nation, no king, no power, no demonic force, and no religious system is strong enough to say, "You can't go out" or "You can't go in" when God says do it.

In speaking of the spirits of false prophets, evil spirits, and the spirit of antichrist, John writes, "Ye are of God, little children, and have overcome them: because greater is he that is in you, than he that is in the world" (1 John 4:4). When we walk obediently in the commands of God's Word, God wreaks vengeance upon anyone who withstands us; sometimes it is relatively quickly, and other times it seems that Israel is unduly long-suffering with the wicked. But whether He waits 400 years or merely 40, as in these two examples , God gets His vengeance. As has often been quoted, "The wheels of God grind slowly, but they grind exceedingly fine."

The Purpose of Vengeance

Certainly the purpose of divine vengeance upon the enemies of the Church must be broader than mere judgement or recompense. David poetically suggests that one of the purposes of God's vengeance is "that thy foot may be dipped in the blood of thine enemies, and the tongue of thy dogs in the same" (Psalms 68:23). Being a man of war, David knew well the value of letting the younger men share in the victories of the older. Sometimes the foot soldier knew only the awfulness of the conflict and needed to have an opportunity to share in the elation of victory that comes by being part of the vanquishment of the enemy.

When Joshua was conquering the Promised Land, he was so consistently successful that the kings of Jerusalem, Hebron, Jarmuth, Lachish, and Eglon formed a coalition to first destroy Gibeon for making a league with the Hebrews and then to drive Joshua and his people out of the land. God joined the battle with great hailstones so that ". . . they were more which died with hailstones than they whom the children of Israel slew with the sword" (Joshua 10:11), and then the Lord hearkened to Joshua's plea and caused the sun to stand still ". . . until the people had avenged themselves upon their enemies . . ." (Joshua 10:13). As the battle turned against them, "these five kings fled, and hid themselves in a cave at Makkedah" (Joshua 10:16). In response to news of this discovery, Joshua instructed that a stone be rolled over the entrance to the cave and that guards be stationed until the battle was over.

When Israel returned from pursuing and slaughtering the armies of these kings, Joshua commanded that the kings be brought out of the caves, and ". . . Joshua called for all the men of Israel, and said unto the captains of the men of war which went with him, Come near, put your feet upon the necks of these kings. . . . And Joshua said unto them, Fear not, nor be dismayed . . . for thus shall the Lord do to all your enemies against whom ye fight. And afterward Joshua smote them, and slew them, and hanged them on five trees . . ." (Joshua 10:24–26).

Recognizing that Joshua is but the Hebrew spelling of the name Jesus, and that both obviously mean "saviour," it is comforting to know that our greater than Joshua, the Lord Jesus Christ Himself, chooses to share His great victory over the five-fold enemy called the devil, satan, the accuser of the brethren, that old serpent, and the dragon, with His people. We are assured that "the God of peace shall bruise Satan under your feet shortly . . ." (Romans 16:20), and that "Thou shalt tread upon the lion and adder: the young lion and the dragon shalt thou trample under feet. (Psalms 91:13). Before God consigns our great enemy into the Lake of Fire He invites His Church to enjoy the feeling of total victory over that enemy. God wants our feet to tramp heavily upon the necks of this enemy so that every fiber of our being can be awakened to the thrill of victory.

This is the purpose of vengeance as it affects the Church. "Sin shall not have dominion over you . . ." (Romans 6:14) is only half of the truth. By being allowed to put our feet on the necks of our enemies, or, as David put it, "That thy foot may be dipped in the blood of thy enemies . . ." (Psalms 68:23), we enter into an experiential awareness that we have dominion over sin. We are not conquered; we are conquerors. The Church is not subject to satan; the devil is subject to the Church. God's people are not victims; we are victors through the Lord Jesus Christ. We enter into His conquest, and we share His victory. He conquers the enemy, and we put our feet on his neck while Christ slays him and hangs him up for all to see. The vengeance is God's; the victory is ours!

Egypt sought to prohibit Israel's exodus from bondage, and God took vengeance upon her. Bashan tried to prohibit Israel from entering into the Promised Land, and God executed vengeance upon her. These five kings attempted to prevent Israel from possessing her inheritance after entering it, and once again God exacted vengeance. Whether it's by a watery grave or a valley cave, God will control and destroy any enemy that withstands His Church when she seeks to possess her possessions in Christ Jesus. Oh, God gives the enemy every chance to let go without being destroyed, but if he persists, God will release His mighty power in taking vengeance on him. Jesus taught His disciples, "And shall not God avenge his own elect, which cry day and night unto him, though he bear long with them? I tell you that he will avenge them speedily . . ." (Luke 18:7,8).

God is an avenging God, and today's generation would do well to believe it. Divine judgement, retribution, and vengeance may be the object of ridicule in today's permissive society, but it is a part of the very nature of God. Sin shall be judged; sinners will be punished; but any enemy that seeks to prevent God's people from coming out of bondage, entering into God's promises, or possessing their possessions will know the fury of God's vengeance. But the Church will see God promenading before her as her King and her Priest.

9
God Promenading

They have seen thy goings, O God; even the goings of my God, my King, in the sanctuary. The singers went before, the players on instruments followed after; among them were the damsels playing with timbrels.

PSALMS 68:24,25

In the days of Moses the watchmen's cry, "Let God arise" set in motion a gigantic procession in the wilderness as priests and Levites followed the moving cloud, and the entire camp of Israel followed them from one campsite to another. It was an awesome parade of magnificent proportions that often struck terror in the heart of surrounding nations.

Similarly, the occasion for which David wrote this psalm was also a lengthy and colorful procession, led by King David himself, as the Ark of the Lord of all the earth was returned to Jerusalem with pomp and circumstance. David could not conceive God's goings as being private or common, for as king he had become accustomed to the constant entourage that surrounded him and to the special attention that was given to him in state processions. He refused to visualize God's movements at a lesser level, she wrote, and probably sang, "Your procession has come into view, O God, the procession of my God and King into the sanctuary. In front are the singers, after them the musicians; with them are the maidens playing tambourines" (Psalms 68:24,25 NIV).

The Procession in This Promenade

The Hebrew word David chose to use for "goings" is *halikah*, which literally means "a walking, a procession, a march, or a company." Although this is the only time this word is used in the entire Bible, it was chosen carefully, for it aptly describes what David was demonstrating: God promenading in the midst of His people. It was God on display, God at the head of a parade commemorating Him. It seems that in modern religion God is seldom put on display; He isn't expected to show Himself, and it certainly is not anticipated that He would go anywhere if He did not show Himself. The "ways" of the Lord that were made known to Moses (*see* Psalms 103:7), and the "goings" of God that were so enjoyed by David, are all too often ignored, rejected, or spurned by today's religionists, but refusing to know does not invalidate truth. There are "goings" of God; God does march in regal procession among His Church. While we may be unable to produce these goings, we are urged to participate in them, for God invites us to promenade with Him.

That man was created for fellowship with God is widely proclaimed throughout the Scriptures. In Eden's garden God used to walk with Adam as they discussed the marvelous world and everything that God had put in it. Although they named the plants and the animals together, the purpose of these daily walks was less for the dissemination of knowledge and more for fellowship. God was enjoying the companionship of His highest-ranked creatures, and He was teaching Adam and Eve the joys of walking with God. It may well have begun as a very small procession, but sanctified imagination can easily visualize the animals joining in the parade, for they had never had occasion to fear either God or man.

As time moved on, man multiplied, but sin mutilated this pure relationship with the Almighty God, so God made a provision, through the sacrificial system, for man to be reunited to intimate fellowship. "Enoch walked with God: and he was not; for God took him" (Genesis 5:24), and Noah so walked with God as to enjoy a hobby together with God – boat building! Abraham was called to walk out of Ur of the Chaldees "unto a land that I will shew thee" (Genesis 12:1), and many generations later Moses would lead over 4 million of Abraham's seed back into this inheritance.

This walking with God that had been preserved in individuals was extended to families and nations. For instance, Abraham was chosen because God knew ". . . that he will command his children and his household after him and they shall keep the way of the Lord . . ." (Genesis 18:19), and the progeny of priests, and later of the kings, were divided into those who "walked in the ways of the Lord" (*see* Deuteronomy 5:33). As Israel becme a monarchial nation, her kings were approved or disapproved by God according to whether or not they walked in the ways of God. In times of battle these kings – both the approved and the disapproved – always considered God as leading them into the fray, and frequently God dramatically demonstrated that indeed the entire military encounter had been a promenade in which God led His people to an amazing victory.

This concept did not stop at the completion of the Old Testament canon, for Jesus began His ministry by calling a group of men to march through Israel with Him, and often such multitudes of people joined this procession as to force Christ out of the cities into the uninhabited areas. The triumphal entry of Christ into Jerusalem and the subsequent march down the Via Dolorosa bearing His cross were high promenadings.

The leaders of the early Church seemed to visualize themselves as being participants in a parade, for they expected the risen Christ to lead them in their stand before magistrates, in their missionary ventures, in their public preaching of the Gospel, and even in the daily decisions of life. It is not surprising, then, that in their writings they urged the believers, "as ye have therefore received Christ Jesus the Lord, *so walk ye in him*" (Colossians 2:6, italics added), and to ". . . walk in the Spirit, and ye shall not fulfil the lust of the flesh" (Galatians 5:16). As a matter of fact, the Christian life is spoken of as a "walk" well over thirty-five times in the New Testament, for our salvation is not pictured as a doctrinal position but as a progressive life of following the Lord. The truly born-again believer finds himself in a promenade that stretches from earth to heaven and which encompasses so great a multitude that John could not even hazard a guess as to its size when he saw them parading in heaven (Revelation 7:9). Surely "they have seen Thy procession, O God, the procession of my God, my King, into the sanctuary" (Psalms 68:24 MLB).

The Participants in This Promenade

This is the third time in Psalm 68 that David speaks of God's procession. In verse one he cried, "Let God arise," which signaled the movement of Israel's camps in a parade behind God. In verse seven he says ". . . thou wentest forth," followed with a listing of seven things that happened when God marched on. In this twenty-fourth verse David again proclaims God's promenade, and, as in the other references, assures us that God doesn't march alone; He leads a vast host of rejoicing people who celebrate His presence and guidance in mirth, music, and marching.

Like the circus parade of yesterday that both announced the arrival of the tented show and gave a preview of what was in store under the "big top," God enjoys parading through a community displaying the trophies of His grace to the bystanders and sharing a minute demonstration of what is available to those who love His appearing. The redeemed men, the rejoicing women, the reclaimed dregs of society, and the romantic dancers may form a spectacle as unearthly and unusual as the trained circus performers, but there is an undeniable aura of happines and awareness that is, of itself, both impressive and attractive. Before His ascension Jesus said, ". . . ye shall be witnesses unto me . . ." (Acts 1:8).

Paul likens our participation in God's promenade to the "triumph" voted for a successful general of Rome who paraded through the triumphal arch with a great host of conquered foes all carrying censers filled with incense. "But thanks be to God," he wrote, "who continually leads us about, captives in Christ's triumphal procession, and everywhere uses us to reveal and spread abroad the fragrance of the knowledge of himself! We are indeed the incense offered by Christ to God, both for those who are on the way to salvation, and for those who are on the way to perdition: to the latter it is a deadly fume that kills, to the former a vital fragrance that brings life" (2 Corinthians 2:14–16 NEB).

It is not angels marching in God's promenade; it is the likes of you and me – humans whose lives have been radically affected by the love of God and their love for God. The Modern Language Bible describes them as "singers in the van, musicians in the rear, in the center maidens playing on timbrels" (Psalms 68:25). These are singing saints who are celebrating God, children of God unashamedly and exorbitantly expressing their ecstatic delight in God's presence. With their attention riveted exclusively upon God, they march with song, shouts, special instrumental music, and dances of delight. Although many of the religious individuals whose attention is generally focused upon themselves may criticize such display of pleasure, the psalmist assures us that God "taketh pleasure in his people . . ." (Psalms 149:4). The expressed emotion of joy and the sight of love being poured out are occasionally offensive to the non-participant, but they delight the heart of God, and that is all that matters, for it is improbable that anything on earth can delight the purely religious person anyway. Textbook Christians will never understand David's invitation to ". . . taste and see that the Lord is good . . ." (Psalms 34:8), but "tasting" saints have found their delight in the Lord, and that delight must be expressed to be fully savored, much as the house dog goes through multiple wagging gyrations in expressing the inner joy produced by the return of his master. Let none condemn the musicians, singers, and dancers who have learned to release their joy in the presence of their saving God, for it would delight the heart of God if all of us would join them in their adulation and outpoured love to Father God. We do not need more restrictions; we need far more release! Parades of sad, sombre, and solemn people rarely attract a crowd of potential participants any more than vinegar attracts flies, but the sweetness of God's love released by His people is almost irresistable to men in today's depressed society.

The Performance in This Promenade

God goes forth in the midst of the praises of His people. After David announced that God was beginning to arise and that His enemies were being scattered, he issued an inspired command to those who would be marching with God. "But let the righteous be glad; let them rejoice before God," David wrote, "yea, let them exceedingly rejoice. Sing unto God, sing praises to his name; extol him that rideth upon the heavens by his name JAH, and rejoice before him" (Psalms 68:3,4).

Quite obviously, then, God not only inhabits the praises of His people (*see* Psalms 22:3), but His goings are in the praises of His people. Praise is a prescribed performance for those who would march with God in His processional, and since this promenading of God is a public display, the accompanying praises would also be public. Too frequently we restrict praise to a private practice while ruling out a public and united performance, but the Scriptures abound with commands for congregational response in praise. David wrote, "I will declare thy name unto my brethren: in the midst of the congregation will I praise thee" (Psalms 22:22), and when this is quoted in Hebrews 2:12 it becomes the voice of our Lord Jesus Christ speaking. Surely if He found it necessary to praise the name of the Father in the congregation, we cannot find a valid excuse for not doing so. It is sad that people will follow the Lord in water baptism and not follow Him in congregational praise and worship, for where have we been granted the option of choosing what to follow and what to fault?

Another psalmist combined a command with a commitment when he wrote, "Praise ye the Lord. I will praise the Lord with my whole heart, in the assembly of the upright, and in the congregation" (Psalms 111:1). Nothing is said about a secret chamber or inner closet; he's committed to expressing praise in the assembly of the congregation, just as Psalms 149:1 commands: "Praise ye the Lord. Sing unto the Lord a new song, and his praise in the congregation of the saints."

Repeatedly the psalms call for united congregational praise, such as "I will give thee thanks in the great congregation: I will praise thee among much people" (Psalms 35:18), or "My foot standeth in an even place: in the congregations will I bless the Lord" (Psalms 26:12), and "Bless ye God in the congregations, even the Lord . . ." (Psalms 68:12).

But the psalms do not hold a monopoly on congregational response to God. Every major Bible division either commands, describes, or exemplifies united praise, as when "David said to all the congregation, Now bless the Lord your God. And all the congregation blessed the Lord God of their fathers, and bowed down their heads and worshipped the

Lord . . ." (1 Chronicles 29:20). Hundreds of years later, and on the other side of the cross, Paul reminded the Ephesian church "that we should be to the praise of his glory, who first trusted in Christ" (Ephesians 1:12); while Peter wrote, "But ye are a chosen generation, a royal priesthood, an holy nation, a peculiar people; that ye should shew forth the praises of him who hath called you out of darkness into his marvelous light" (1 Peter 2:9). Praise was never intended to be merely the private action of a demonstrative person; it is expected to be the public practice of saints who have elected to follow their Lord wherever He may choose to lead them. Is there any other kind of saint in the Bible?

The praise performance spoken of in connection with God's promenading is a melodious praise – praise that is sung to the accompaniment of musical instruments and tambourines. At the dedication of Solomon's temple we read, "It came even to pass, as the trumpeters and singers were as one to make one sound to be heard in praising and thanking the Lord; and when they lifted up their voice with the trumpets and cymbals and instruments of musick, and praised the Lord, saying, For he is good; for his mercy endureth for ever: that then the house was filled with a cloud, even the house of the Lord; So that the priests could not stand to minister by reason of the cloud: for the glory of the Lord had filled the house of God" (2 Chronicles 5:13,14). It was when the instrumentalists, singers, and praisers were so united in their expression of praise that God's glory appeared in the temple in magnificence.

Much later, under Hezekiah's reinstitution of the temple worship, he celebrated the Passover, "And all the congregation worshipped, and the singers sang, and the trumpeters sounded: and all this continued until the burnt offering was finished" (2 Chronicles 29:28). Music is a magnificent vehicle for the inspiration and implementation of praise that will create an atmosphere in which God will move, for God seldom moves among a people who will not praise, but wherever He moves, praise accompanies Him. The Book of Revelation not only repeatedly declares God worthy to be praised, but regularly demonstrates praise to be the normal atmosphere of heaven: angels praise Him; elders praise Him; saints praise Him; and all creation praises the King of Kings. Surely, then, the Church on earth must also enter into a rejoicing praise if she is to be in the retinue of this great King.

In speaking of the "goings of my . . . king" David may have been thinking of the ceremonial coronation of a king, which always abounded with music and praise, or he may have thought of the king in his role as the protector of his people by leading them forth to battle. In Jehoshaphat's day God instructed him to send the singers and praisers to precede the army into a decisive battle (*see* 2 Chronicles 20). Unorthodox as it was, Jehoshaphat obeyed, and God so discomforted the enemy through the ringing shout of songs and praise that they set themselves on a course of self-destruction, making it unnecessary for Judah's army to fight. The choir won the war; the army merely collected the booty. God's ways may seem strange, but they are excellent strategy that always works.

Song can be worship; music should be worship. They are a high form of praise responding to the presence of the King among us as we either coronate Him or follow Him into battle. Of course He has an army called the "heavenly host," but we need not see it in action if we sing in faith, for praise-filled songs break forth into victory as our God goes upon our praise. He, our King, goes upon our song. This was so important to God that an entire division of the priesthood was set aside just for music ministry, both vocal and instrumental (*see* 1 Chronicles 15). These were the first "ministers of music," and their appointment was by divine inspiration.

The last thing any king wants in his entourage is a bunch of bawling, squalling, sniffing, guilt-ridden people whose only song is a funeral song, and who, having religiously done the "right thing," leave the service feeling as miserable as when they came. God our King wants His people to be a joy-filled people, because He forgave our sin, removed our guilt, and imparted His own joy to us. We are encouraged to delight ourselves in the Lord, in His law, and in His Spirit. We are challenged to sing unto the Lord, to praise the Lord, and to magnify and extol the Lord in worshipful song, for this is the expected performance in God's procession.

The Purpose of the Promenade

That God has a purpose for everything He does goes without saying, so it is to be expected that this divine promenade has as its object something greater than the mere release of emotional ecstasy and exuberance. The Living Bible says, "The procession of God my King moves onward to the sanctuary . . ." (Psalms 68:24). No matter where the procession begins, it ends in God's sanctuary, for all of God's processions end there. "Thy way, O God, is in the sanctuary . . ." Asaph wrote in Psalms 77:13. We miss the deeper truth in emphasizing that "God has come down . . ." when actually God's promenade is *from* earth *into* the heavens, just as Jacob's ladder and Jesus' affirmation to Nathanael teach that the angels of God *ascend* and *descend* (*see* John 1:51). The intervention of God in our lives is always to cause us to ascend into His presence, for God's love is an ascending love that reaches the lower and lifts it to the higher. The divine order is always to move from the natural to the spiritual, from the terrestrial to the celestial, and from man to God; and that move is often in the form of a promenade.

God's Word clearly teaches us that the dwelling place of God – His sanctuary – is a locale unknown and undiscoverable by men: "He that dwelleth in the secret place of the most High shall abide under the shadow of the Almighty"

(Psalms 91:1). Since all secret places have secret doors, and unless the Father draws us in we will never successfully enter His realized presence, God marches us from our realm into His realm, knowing that we would never find our way into the divine presence unguided.

The way into God's presence may be as unknown to us as the route through the wilderness was unknown to Moses, but with God as our Guide we cannot fail to arrive at our desired haven. Having exchanged a program for a Person and a map for a Guide, there is no need for tension and worry as we wend our way down life's path, for the responsibility for the entire itinerary is His, not ours. Therefore we can relax, rejoice, and respond to His presence with music, song, and praise. What some religionists have described as a painful and lonely pilgrimage should actually be a praise-filled procession of promenading people reveling in the presence of their God and King: . . . the singers in front, the minstrels last, between them maidens playing timbrels" (Psalms 68:25 RSV).

If we insist upon the painful pilgrimage, we will find our journey taxing, tiring, and tedious, but if we will join God's promcnade with rejoicing and singing, we will discover that God's presence is a strengthening force that renews us.

10
God Strengthening

Thy God hath commanded thy strength: strengthen, O God, that which thou hast wrought for us.

PSALMS 68:28

In viewing the grand procession marching in God's promenade, singing, "Bless ye God in the congregations, even the Lord, from the fountain of Israel (Psalms 68:26), David sees the various tribes of Israel marching behind their God. "The little tribe of Benjamin leads the way. The princes and elders of Judah, and the princes of Zebulun and Naphtali are right behind" (Psalms 68:27 TLB).

It is both a melodious and a majestic occasion. Israel is now settled in the land, organized into self-leadership, and preparing to become a world power. Still, to David it all seems manifestly fragile. Israel had indeed grown strong compared to her former weaknesses, but was this strength sufficient when compared to the hostile forces that surrounded her? "Let God arise," David seems to call "Summon your might; display your strength, O God, for you have done such mighty things for us" (Psalms 68:28 TLB). "What we could not produce, we surely cannot perpetuate," David implies. "Protect us, O God; perpetuate what you have begun."

When we march with God in the wilderness, totally dependent upon Him for food, water, guidance and protection, there is little danger of pride or self-sufficiency, but when we have followed God into the Land of Promise and have shared with Him in victories over our enemies while settling into the land on a permanent basis, it is easy to think that all of this came to pass because of our strength and might. Security and self-sufficiency often produce attitudes of ability that are far more fable than fact. Being planted of the Lord in the midst of His promises should not make us independent of God; it should only make us aware that ". . . he which hath begun a good work in you will perform it until the day of Jesus Christ" (Philippians 1:6), and that ". . . having begun in the Spirit, are ye now made perfect by the flesh?" (Galatians 3:3).

If we enter a realm by God's power, we must continue to exist in that power, for our inability to capture is equally an inability to contain. How rarely do denominations maintain this posture. Somehow once they get things organized they seem to feel that they have matured to the point that they do not need the manifest presence of God leading them any further. We all fail to allow for God promenading in the land; we expect it only in the wilderness. Yet all of us are *who* we are and *where* we are because of the intervention of Christ into our lives. The moment we remove Him from the equation of life, we will quickly degenerate to what we were before Christ came into our lives in the first place. Since it was His power that lifted us, it must be that same power that continues to lift us. Although we are expected to mature in Christ Jesus, we will never mature to a place where we can survive without His presence and power; we will always be dependent upon Him, "for in him we live, and move, and have our being . . ." (Acts 17:28).

The God of the Strength

This is not something that we learn by costly experience; it is a principle laid down by God Himself. He knows better than we do that we are incapable of maintaining any spiritual territory into which He has brought us, so He remains among us as a strengthening force. "Thy God hath commanded thy strength . . ." (Psalms 68:28), David said. Obviously it is "thy God" who does the commanding of the strength. It is not the God of our concepts but the God of divine revelation. Our strength to live the Christian life and to occupy the territory He has conquered for us comes from the Almighty God, here called by His Hebrew name, *Elohim*. ". . . The Lord is the strength of my life; of whom shall I be afraid?" (Psalms 27:1) David asks, and then he affirms, "The Lord will give strength unto his people . . ." (Psalms 29:11). Over and over again the Bible affirms that God is indeed the source of our strength.

It is noteworthy that David does not concern himself or us with the strength of God until he has unfolded multiple pictures of the God of this strength. We have seen God revealed as our Father, our Leader, our Commander in Chief in time of war, our Sustainer, the One who chastens us and who avenges us of our enemies, and as the One who leads the promenade into His sanctuary. We have seen God as able, active, adept, and available. We've learned something of His strength in seeing Him as the Father bringing His children into security, equity, unity, and liberty. We experienced His plenteous provision in His leadings through the wilderness and into the Promised Land. We marveled at His might as He warred against His enemies with His Word, and we thrilled at His presence as we saw Him abiding among men. We perceived His patience in the way He sustained us in our daily trials, and we responded to His love as His chastening hand urged us back into the covenants we had made with Him. We discovered something of His awesome power as we watched Him discharge vengeance upon His enemies, and we marveled at His majesty as He promenaded down the mainstream of life. It is *this* God, this very same God, who has commanded our strength. If He could do all of those things, sharing, strength with us is but a small matter.

"Thy God hath commanded thy strength. . . ." But the strength and the God are inseparable; God's strength is not available apart from His person and presence. The pompous procession of God's promenade led into the sanctuary. Standing there in the manifest presence of his saving God, David cried, "Power belongs to God! His majesty shines down on Israel; his strength is mighty in the heavens. What awe we feel, kneeling here before him in the sanctuary. The God of Israel gives strength and mighty power to his people. Blessed be God!" (Psalms 68:34,35 TLB). It is in the sanctuary that God shares His strength and power; while we worship, God works divine strength into our being. God's strength is not so much conferred as it is shared. When we are yoked together with Him, His strength overcomes our weakness, and His ability compensates for our inability. "I can do all things through Christ which strengtheneth me" (Philippians 4:13), Paul declared. He does not affirm that he can do anything because of Christ's strength, but he couples strength and performance with the strength of Christ's presence: ". . . *through* Christ . . ." Jesus sought to make this crystal clear to His disciples, and to us, when He told them, ". . . without me [apart from me] ye can do nothing" (John 15:5). We are never given an enablement that can function when we are severed from Christ Jesus our Lord, for He is the Vine; we are but the branches. The life-giving force flows through Him into us, enabling us to bring forth fruit as long as we remain intimately related to Him. While this deep-seated relationship remains, "Thy God hath commanded thy strength." It is a living outgrowth of an affectionate abiding.

God Commands Our Strength

The expression "Thy God hath *commanded* thy strength . . ." (Psalms 68:28) cannot mean that we have some strength and that God is commanding us to use it, or that

God is taking command of the use of it, for inherently we have no strength that God can command. Before Calvary, the world, the flesh, and the devil sapped all spiritual strength from us. Since our conversion the pressures of daily life and the repeated conflicts with the tempter continually exhaust the limited life supply that was imparted at the cross. Eventually we have to learn that we have nothing to gain in trying to draw from nervous energy, for we cannot draw strength from nonexistent inner resources. God, who knows us better than we know ourselves, would never command us to be strong, when He knows we have no inner strength from which to draw. David wrote, "For he knoweth our frame; he remembereth that we are dust" (Psalms 103:14).

Far from suggesting that God demands us to function in nonexistent strength, this verse offers us strength from an outside source. The Hebrew word that we have translated "command" is *tsavah*, which has at least four meanings: "to send the messenger; to appoint; to give charge; to put in order." Each shade of meaning enhances the picture of God imparting strength to us. God has appointed strength for His people; He has given a charge that all needed strength shall be appropriated, and that strength has already been put in order – it is arranged for us in such a manner that we can receive it and respond with it – for God has already done everything that is necessary to make power available to His children here on the earth. It is far less our reaching out and up for that power and more God reaching out and down with the strength.

The concept of God appointing a messenger to bring strength to His people is consistent with the teaching of Scriptures, for repeatedly God dispatched angels to help men in times of weakness. We are taught that the angels are ". . . all ministering spirits, sent forth to minister for them who shall be heirs of salvation" (Hebrews 1:14), and then from the vision of Jacob's ladder to the conclusion of the

Book of Revelation we see them on missions from God to man. When God Himself became man and underwent such resistance against sin as to produce sweat of blood in the garden of Gethsemane, "there appeared an angel unto him from heaven, strengthening him" (Luke 22:43). God the Father commanded strength for His Son, and that strength was delivered by an angel. Since Jesus was man and used only the power, authority, and provision that are available to men, it should not be considered too unusual for God to commission an angel to strengthen believers in this day. "God hath sent a messenger with strength" is an allowable paraphrase of Psalms 68:28.

Back in the fifties when I was pastoring in eastern Washington, I experienced a time of discouragement and great frustration. I was teaching in a Bible school, pastoring a church, working five hours a day in commercial radio, and demonstrating organs for a music store. I asked God for permission to withdraw from the ministry and accept a job as manager of a music store. God agreed to my decommissioning inasmuch as I had already spent more time in the ministry than He ever required of an Old Testament priest; but He told me that although I would prosper in business, I would have leanness of soul, so I hastily withdrew my request. This conversation with God took place on a Sunday afternoon and left me so introspective and ashamed that I dreaded having to conduct the evening service.

Nothing I did in that evening service seemed to go well; we merely went through our religious ritual without any sense of the presence of God whatever. However, as I began to preach that evening I was aware of an energy that was far beyond me. I preached with authority, illumination, and inspiration greater than I had experienced in my ministry up to that time. The congregation sensed a fresh anointing and they responded to the altar call almost as one man, with the exception of one lady who sat in the congregation staring at me without so much as blinking her eyes. Leaving the platform, I walked down to her and said, "Sister, is something wrong?"

"I won't stop looking at you until I see him leave," she responded.

"What are you talking about?" I said.

"I happened to have my eyes open while you were praying before your sermon," she said, "and I saw an angel from the Lord come down and step behind you and then step right into you, and he hasn't left yet. I want to see him when he goes."

Only then did I understand what had happened in my preaching. God had commanded strength. God had appointed strength; He had sent a messenger with both strength for me and a message for the congregation. I'm confident that far more frequently than we know, God's commissioned angels come among us to touch, strengthen, and communicate the Word of God, for the Bible declares that Moses got the Law from angels acting as God's mouthpiece (*see* Galatians 3:19 and Acts 7:53).

On repeated occasions during conference ministries throughout the world I have had people tell me that they have seen an angel standing behind, or alongside me, or step inside me when I have been preaching. Happily, God still commands His strength when and where it is needed, and frequently that strength comes in the form of a messenger sent from heaven.

"Thy God – hath commanded – thy *strength*" (Psalms 68:28), and the Hebrew word we have translated "strength" is *'owz* (or *oz*), which is translated seven different ways in the King James Bible. Its most frequent translation is "strength" (sixty times) and "strong" (seventeen times), for this is the fundamental thrust of the word. Other times it is translated as "might," "mighty," "power," "boldness," and "loud." "Thy God hath commanded thy strength, power, might, and boldness." Sometimes this comes to us through angelic action, but always it is an outgrowth of the authority of God's Word. God entered into a legal agreement with us; He made us beneficiaries in His will when He established the New Testament. We read, "For a testament is of force after men are dead: otherwise it is of no strength at all while the testator liveth" (Hebrews 9:17), and it was at the Last Supper, just before His death, that Jesus declared, ". . . This cup is the new testament in my blood, which is shed for you" (Luke 22:20). In effect, Jesus said, "My death shall release to the believer all that I have pledged and promised unto him. When this will is probated 'the works that I do shall he do also; and greater works than these shall he do; because I go unto my Father'" (*see* John 14:12). There is no greater strength available to any of us than the strength of the testament of the Word of God. Whether our puny minds can conceive and understand the Word or not. God's strength is in His Word, and its promises do not stand on our experience but upon God's person, ". . . for thou hast magnified thy word above all thy name" (Psalms 138:2).

The strength of a divine commission coupled with divine capability gives us great boldness in service, and this word *oz* is translated as "boldness" elsewhere in our Bible. The coming of the Holy Spirit into our lives can produce a tremendous boldness in formerly timid persons, as is evidenced in Peter's bold sermon on the day of Pentecost. The disciples must have been stunned to see this man who just a few weeks earlier had denied any association with Christ almost brazenly charge the Jews with the crucifixion of the Lord Jesus. Later we see this same Peter sleeping the night before his scheduled execution, and, after his angelic release, dauntlessly and openly preaching Jesus.

It is God's will that we have boldness to face the enemy and boldness to face people, but His perfect will is to have boldness to come into the presence of God. Speaking of Christ Jesus our Lord, Paul wrote, "In whom we have boldness and access with confidence by the faith of him" (Ephesians 3:12), and "Let us therefore come boldly unto the throne of grace, that we may obtain mercy, and find grace to help in time of need" (Hebrews 4:16). God has commanded the strength of boldness – boldness to come into the presence of God. This courage of rights granted to us, of authority vested in us, and of a relationship into which we have entered, is a strength God has commissioned to us, ". . . for he hath said, I will never leave thee, no forsake thee. So that we may boldly say, The Lord is my helper, and I will not fear what man shall do unto me" (Hebrews 13:5,6).

The third most frequent word used to translate *oz* is "might." God has commanded might to those who have followed Him through the wilderness into the Land of Promise. In Paul's prayer for the Ephesian Christians he said, "For this cause I bow my knees unto the Father of our Lord Jesus Christ. . . . that he would grant you, according to the riches of his glory, to be strengthened with might by his Spirit in the inner man" (Ephesians 3:14,16), and in praying for the Colossian brothers and sisters he prayed, ". . . that ye might be . . . strengthened with all might, according to his glorious power . . ." (Colossians 1:9,11). What is the measurement Paul uses in praying that we be strenghtened with *all might*? All of the resources, strengths, and might of heaven are to be made available to weak, feeble humans like you and me. Can we handle this might of heaven, the might of God's angels, the might of His faith, the might of His love, the might of His Word, the might of His name, the might of His blood, the might of His Church, the might of His Body, and the might of His presence? With all of this available to us, how dare we testify that "we are serving God in our own weak way?"

When we genuinely need might, God commissions it to us by way of an angelic messenger, an anointing of the Holy Spirit, an illumination of the Word, or through a brother or sister in the Body, but we always receive all that we need if not much more than we need.

It is meekness, not weakness, that God desires in our lives. It is strength, not strivings, that He has commanded to be made available to us. God will never com mission a task that is beyond His ability to perform through us, and He always makes both legal and practical strength available to us in Christian service, as is illustrated when Jesus "called his twelve disciples together, and gave them power and authority over all devils, and to cure diseases" (Luke 9:1). He gave them both "power" (Greek: *dunamis*, meaning "ability") and "authority" (Greek: *exousia*, meaning "right or authority"), for a commision without capability is a mockery. God has not merely commanded our service; He has equally commanded our strength!

In his *Exhaustive Concordance of the Bible*, James Strong says that the Hebrew word *'owz* (his spelling) means to "strengthen in various applications (force; security; majesty; praise)." God not only strengthens us in the sense of spiritual force that makes our ministry effective; He also strengthens us in the area of security. Peter declares that we "are kept by the power of God through faith unto salvation ready to be revealed in the last time" (1 Peter 1:5). The security of the believer is the strength of God made available to him far more than it is the faith of the believer in the God of that strength. We have been called by God, cleansed, and commissioned by God, and we will also be kept by the power of God. Great is our security, and great is the strength that this security gives to the believer!

Dr. Strong also suggests that the word *'owz* can refer to being strengthened in majesty and praise. We, as "kings and priests unto God" (Revelation 1:6), are allowed to share in the majesty of Almighty God. As we sit with Him in heavenly places, and as we promenade with Him through earthly habitations, we are invited to share in His glory, majesty, and praise. Just as the wife of our president shares in his majesty and praise, so the believers who are called "the bride of Christ" share in the majestic splendor of our heavenly Bridegroom, who happens to be "King of Kings, and Lord of Lords" (Revelation 19:16). Technically, no glory, honor, majesty, or praise is due us, but because of our close association and our intimate relationship to God, we find ourselves sharing in His glory, honor, majesty, and praise, which is endless and enduring. God strengthens us by sharing some of His majesty with us, for "Honour and majesty are before him: strength and beauty are in his sanctuary" (Psalms 96:6).

God Solidifies His Work

In applying this to his own nation, David followed this divine commitment of strength with a personal plea: ". . . strengthen, O God, that which thou hast wrought for us" (Psalms 68:28). To those of us who read the English Bible it would appear that David is merely pleading a promise, but those who have a working knowledge of the Hebrew language recognize immediately that David has used an entirely different word for "strengthen" than he used for "strength." He uses the word *'azaz*, which not only means "to become or make strong," but it is sometimes translated as "harden." It occurs in Proverbs 21:29 where we read, "A wicked man hardeneth his face . . ." referring, in all probability, to developing a "poker face" so as to hide any inner emotion. It is beautifully illustrated in Pharaoh's repeated hardening of his heart to the pleas and plagues of God upon him and his nation.

"Harden, O God, that which thou hast wrought for us" seems like an unusual plea, but I believe I under stand David's prayer, for I have seen so much of what God has done in the lives of the people disappear in the hour of temptation. The translators of the Amplified Bible catch sight of this nuance of meaning, for they translte this verse, "Your God has commanded your strength [your might in

His service and impenetrable hardness to temptation] . . ."
(Psalms 68:28 AMPLIFIED). God can so strengthen the lives
of His followers that they become rock hard to temptation.

Perhaps God's strength is somewhat akin to liquid Jell-O
that is poured into a mold. Until it has set or hardened, it
cannot be served. God pours His strength into us like mixed
concrete, intending that it take the form and shape of our
lives, but unless it hardens it has no strength or utility.
"Strengthen, O God. . . ." Cause Thy strength within us to
set; harden Thy work within us until it takes a settled, firm
course of faith that will not be deterred by fear, emotion, or
doubt.

As Paul told the Christians in Corinth, "Therefore, my
beloved brethren, be ye steadfast, unmoveable, always
abounding in the work of the Lord, forasmuch as ye know
that your labour is not in vain in the Lord" (Corinthians
15:58). God's strength need not be transient or temporary,
for God can harden it until it is a permanent fixture in our
lives, enabling us to be steadfast, unmoveable, and resistant
to temptation.

The word most frequently used by the translators of the
King James Bible to interpret the Hebrew word 'azaz is
"prevail." "Prevail, O God . . ." is David's plea. Jesus
assured us that ". . . upon this rock I will build my church;
and the gates of hell shall not prevail against it" (Matthew
16:18), which certainly means, then, that the Church shall
prevail over hell itself! There have been times in history
when it temporarily seemed that hell was prevailing over
God's Church, but God assures us that the devil will never
prevail and the Church cannot fail, for the strength that our
God has commanded is strength that will triumph! We do
not lay God's strength alongside our failures and declare,
"The strength didn't work." We do better to lay our failures
alongside God's strength and declare that had we appropriated that strength, we would never have failed. Paul
expected God's strength to succeed, for he wrote, "Being

confident of this very thing, that he which hath begun a good work in you will perform it until the day of Jesus Christ" (Philippians 1:6). God never begins a program He is unable to complete. If He shares strength with the people of His hand who inhabit His land, that strength will prevail over every obstacle, opposition, and enemy, for ". . . greater is he that is in you, than he that is in the world" (1 John 4:4).

God Strengthens His Work, Not Necessarily Ours

This provision, pledge, and plea for strengthening is totally concerned with ". . . that which thou has wrought for us" (Psalms 68:28). So many times we plead for God to strengthen something that He never began in the first place and in which He has never been involved. Somehow we feel that no matter what the beginning may be or the involvements may have become, if we can just contact God, God will strengthen it. We sit for hours and days in committee sessions making our plans and at the final dismissal ask God to bless and strengthen them, but we have a right to ask God to strengthen only what He has wrought. God is not in the business of strengthening the works of our hands, the products of our flesh, the glories of our spirits, or the abilities of our minds; He has merely pledged to strengthen what He is doing.

How imperative it is then, for us to find out what God is doing and to get involved with God rather than to get involved in activities and then try to get God to give us a little strength in which to move. We do not have a right to claim the promises of God for everything we set out to do or to depend upon the strength of God to carry out selfish ambitions, but we do have a right to cry, "Thy God hath commanded thy strength; strengthen, O God, that which thou has wrought for us" (Psalms 68:28). When we are involved with Him in daily living or in ministry, we can expect Him to strengthen us, to harden our work to where it takes form, to enable us to prevail against the enemy, and to give sufficient strength that our lives will accomplish what God has purposed that they achieve.

This strengthening God, who brings His Church to spiritual maturity and continues to be the source of her life while she resides here on earth, not only completely preserves what He has done in, for, and through the Church, but He sets Himself up in His holy temple to rule and reign over the entire world. He strengthens us while He wields the scepter over them, for His sovereignty is equal over the Church and over the world. When it is submitted to, it becomes strength; when it is resisted, it becomes compulsion.

11
God Reigning

Because of thy temple at Jerusalem shall kings bring presents unto thee. Rebuke the company of spearmen, the multitude of the bulls, with the calves of the people, till every one submit himself with pieces of silver: scatter thou the people that delight in war. Princes shall come out of Egypt; Ethiopia shall soon stretch out her hands unto God.
PSALMS 68:29–31

By this point in the psalm the procession that had taken the Ark of the Lord from Obed-edom with such pomp and ceremony has now ended in the capital city of Jerusalem, and already David is envisioning a permanent temple as God's residence. His cry "because of thy temple at Jerusalem shall kings bring presents unto thee" (Psalms 68:29) is the expression of a strong desire released in audible prayer that the Temple may become the zenith and Jerusalem the metropolis of the world. "Let God arise," David seemed to say, "and let the world bow at His feet in His holy Temple at Jerusalem."

Perhaps this could be dismissed as ambitious thinking, for under the mighty hand of God, David had pretty well conquered the nations that surrounded Israel, and Jerusalem was indeed the capital of the world he knew; but David was far more than a king – he was a prophet of God who not only heard from God but frequently spoke forth on God's behalf. It is almost to be expected, then, that what he was enjoying historically – the reign of God over Israel and surrounding nations – would be expanded prophetically to encompass the vision of God ruling over all the nations of the earth. Although a great patriot, David quite consistently saw Jehovah as the God of the entire world. Although he did not see a replacement of Judaism, he saw it encompassing the Gentiles as well as the Jews. To David, God was the sovereign ruler of all the earth – none were exempt from His authority. David's revelational songs seemed to be the theme of the prophets who also declared the Lordship of God over all people.

The author of the Book of Hebrews, in speaking of God in the form of Jesus, wrote, "Thou hast put all things in subjection under his feet . . . he left nothing that is not put under him. But now we see not yet all things put under him. But we see Jesus . . ." (Hebrews 2:8,9). All things are in subjection to God and His Christ, but at the present time this is not completely manifested to our natural eyes and understanding.

God Reigning in Individual Lives

While David desired and envisioned the universal rule of God over this earth, he did not know that God would effect this by starting with individuals, enlarging it to the Church, and eventually expanding it to the nations of the world. God is *now* King over all the earth. He whom John the revelator saw as "Faithful and True . . ." whose name ". . . is called The Word of God . . ." right now ". . . hath on his vesture and on his thigh a name written, KING OF KINGS, AND LORD OF LORDS" (Revelation 19:11,13,16).

When this "Word of God" walked among men, He came ". . . preaching the gospel of the kingdom of God, And saying, The time is fulfilled, and the kingdom of God is at hand . . ." (Mark 1:14,15). This was the consistent theme of Christ's preaching: "The kingdom of God (or of heaven) is at hand." He proclaimed Himself to be their King, and His teaching undeviatingly expressed and expounded the principles of His Kingdom. While the multitude, and even His disciples, expected an immediate overthrow of Roman rule and the reestablishing of a Davidic government in Jerusalem, Jesus quelled all such hopes and dreams by His behaviour after the triumphal entry into Jerusalem and by His subsequent trial and crucifixion. It was not time for the world kingdom; it was God's time to make Himself available to the individual as Lord and King.

When the Pharisees demanded that Jesus tell them when the Kingdom of God should come, Jesus assured them that the Kingdom would not come with outward show, and then declared, ". . . behold, the kingdom of God is within you" (Luke 17:21), suggesting that the reign of Christ today is in the individual hearts and lives of the ones who have submitted to the Lordship of Jesus Christ. The beginning locale of God's Kingdom is you and me. He is sovereign in His saints; He reigns in the redeemed!

Our initial action that brings us into salvation is "if thou shalt confess with thy mouth the Lord Jesus, and shalt believe in thine heart that God hath raised him from the dead, thou shalt be saved" (Romans 10:9). J. B. Phillips translates that first phrase, "If you openly admit by *your own mouth* that Jesus Christ is Lord. . . ." Salvation is not mere belief of historical facts; it is accepting Jesus Christ as our personal Lord and Saviour. It is a renunciation of an old way of life and an enthusiastic embracing of the work, ways, word, and authority of God in our lives. It is the surrender of our wills to His will and the transfer of all rights to ourselves to His sovereignty. As He becomes our Lord we enter into His Kingdom.

How desperately we need to make Jesus the Lord of everything in our lives, from our thoughts through our possessions. Too often we surrender our spirits to His Lordship but reserve our souls and bodies; but as R. A. Torrey used to declare, "Christ will be Lord *of* all or not Lord *at* all." Any area of our lives which we will not bring under the authority of the Lord Jesus Christ is a potential zone of satanic control in the time of crisis. How many Christians have had to answer Christ's call to service with "I would love to go for you, Lord, but I will have to clear up some financial obligations before I can do so." Their insistence upon handling their finances "their way" instead of letting Jesus be Lord of their money incapacitates them for obedience to the call of God.

Others who have successfully answered the call of the Lord into full-time Christian service have found themselves disqualified after years of service because their sexual appetites had never been brought to the cross of the Lord Jesus Christ. They resisted allowing God's Lordship to reign there, fearing that He might make eunuchs out of them, so satan enticed them into extrascriptural use of their sensuality so that instead of being an example of godliness to the believers they became an exhibition of carnality to believers and unbelievers alike.

While we legally enter Christ's Kingdom at Calvary, all of us have many things that belong to the kingdom of self coursing through our systems which direly need to be brought under the control of Jesus Christ the Lord. It is not our love relationship with God that is at stake here, nor is our state of salvation threatened; but God is searching for persons who will rule and reign with Him in His Kingdom, and the Lord gives rule only to those who are ruled. All who would exercise the authority of God must first be surrendered to the authority of God. God can entrust service into our hands only to the extent that we have entrusted ourselves into His hands, for our commission is commensurate with our consecration.

This is curiously illustrated in the lives of David's mighty men. When David was fleeing from Saul and came to the cave Adullam, we read that "every one that was in distress, and every one that was in debt, and every one that was discontented, gathered themselves unto him; and he became a captain over them: and there were with him about four hundred men" (1 Samuel 22:2). For many years these men submitted to David's reign over them, until these former troubled men became David's "mighty men of valor" and were appointed as captains and chiefs of his army – although they were not Hebrews and had no right to these positions. These former cowards became courageous, and these who had been outlaws to one king became leaders for another. The transforming power was the reign of David. And so it is with us, for Christ's reign in our lives transforms us, too.

While the smallest measure of the Kingdom of God is the life of an individual, the quality of God's Kingdom is defined thus: "For the kingdom of God is not meat and drink; but righteousness, and peace, and joy in the Holy Ghost" (Romans 14:17). God's Kingdom is a positive Kingdom that produces righteousness, peace, and joy through the operation of the Holy Spirit. If, then, I have an area of my life that consistently lacks peace, is steeped in misery, and is embroiled in turmoil, I can be pretty well assured that this portion of my life is not yet in God's Kingdom, for His Kingdom is "peace and joy in the Holy Ghost." Being in His Kingdom does not always change my circumstances, but it will greatly alter my reaction to those circumstances. Joy is the trademark of a true Christian; it is the hallmark of God's Kingdom on earth, and it is the heritage of all who submit to that Kingdom. The loss of joy usually indicates the withdrawal of an area of life from the authority of the Lord Jesus Christ; for where He is Lord, there is joy. He Himself said, "These things have I spoken unto you, that my joy might remain in you, and that your joy might be full" (John 15:11).

Surrendering our lives to the Lordship of Jesus is never loss; it is eternal gain. The most relaxing position in all the world is to have another person totally responsible for your actions, needs, training, and guidance, and this is what the Lord Jesus Christ offers to all who enter into His Kingdom. God becomes our Father in such an intimate way that living on earth becomes a delight rather than a duty, our service to God becomes a pleasure rather than pressure, and our relationship to other people in the Kingdom is peaceful rather than provoking.

God Reigning in His Church

While it is proper to think of the Kingdom of God in its smallest proportion – the individual – it becomes obvious that this is but a capsule quantity of the whole. Throughout the Bible the seat of Christ's spiritual authority is called Zion, which, as we have previously seen, is both a poetic and prophetic term for the Church. When we think of the collective group of believers as a Bride, we see Christ as the Husband; when we see them as the Body, we see Christ as both the Head and the animating principle; but when we see the redeemed as a Kingdom, we see Christ as the King ruling and reigning in the midst of them.

In instructing us how to pray, Jesus said, "After this manner therefore pray ye: Our Father which art in heaven, Hallowed be thy name. Thy kingdom come. Thy will be done in earth, as it is in heaven" (Matthew 6:9,10), establishing that just as the heavenly will and the earthly will are to flow as one, so the heavenly Kingdom and the earthly Kingdom are one. The separation is geographic, not genetic; it is the same Kingdom functioning in two realms – the heavenly and the earthly. God is King among His angels, and He is equally King among His saints. His sovereignty in each realm is not subject to the submission of the residents of the Kingdom; it is not dependent upon any response.

Paul had insight into the totality of God's reign in the Church, for he wrote, "Giving thanks unto the Father, . . . Who hath delivered us from the power of darkness, and hath translated us into the kingdom of his dear Son"

(Colossians 1:12,13). Inasmuch as I have devoted an entire chapter to this verse in my recent book *Let Us See Jesus*, I will not repeat myself but will merely quote the first paragraph of that chapter.

> In Paul's day, monarchies were the rule; in our day they are the exception to the rule. Paul understood the authority of a king and the ramifications of a kingdom. Accordingly, he declares that we have not only been delivered out of the power of darkness but "translated . . . into the kingdom of his dear Son." Paul consistently taught that God did not send Jesus Christ merely to save us from sin, but He sent Him to bring us into the Kingdom of heaven. . . . God never lost sight of His original goal to form a "kingdom of priests" (Exodus 19:6), even though Israel rejected the concept and settled for the tribe of Levi as their substitutes, and eventually rejected their unseen God as their king, demanding that one of their own be enthroned as monarch over them. But God's purposes are never changed by man's choices. . . . Although God gave men the desires of their hearts in Saul and subsequent earthly kings, He also gave the prophets insight into the coming divine King – the promised Messiah.

To the Hebrews, the Spirit said, "Wherefore we receiving a kingdom which cannot be moved, let us have grace, whereby we may serve God acceptably with reverence and godly fear" (Hebrews 12:28). The Kingdom is entered by translation, and it remains immovable; it is permanent. Heaven will not reject it, hell cannot remove it, and saints cannot ruin it. It is God's Kingdom in His Church, and He maintains total control over it.

Please be aware that there is often quite a discrepancy between God's Church and the religious system in this world that calls itself the church. Men are religious beings who must worship, and much worship calls for an organized religious system. Organization does not of itself disqualify any group from being members of God's Kingdom, but it is patently possible to organize without being participants in the Kingdom of God.

Some have suggested that the true Church of the Living God will eventually capture the false religious systems, but since Saul's kingdom was never captured – it capitulated – I don't expect God to give the old religious system enough credence to bother fighting it; He is just going to let it die, and those individuals who survive will come to Christ, pleading with Him to reign over them. Actually, the issue has never been religion. The issue has universally been "Who is King?" In the true Church, Jesus Christ is ". . . the blessed and only Potentate, the King of kings, and Lord of lords; Who only hath immortality, dwelling in the light which no man can approach unto; whom no man hath seen, nor can see: to whom be honour and power everlasting. Amen" (1 Timothy 6:15,16).

The New Testament clearly teaches that God, in Christ, is the Head of the Church. ". . . Christ is the head of the church: and he is the saviour of the body. . . . the church is subject unto Christ . . . Christ also loved the church, and gave himself for it; That he might sanctify and cleanse it . . . That he might present it to himself a glorious church, not having spot, or wrinkle, or any such thing; but that it should be holy and without blemish" (Ephesians 5:23–27). If God is its Head, and Christ is its Life, the Church cannot grow weaker and weaker for growing stronger and stronger. God is not going to sneak an emaciated, stunted, feeble, anemic Church out the back door just before the devil kills her off. God is strengthening, enlarging, beautifying, and purifying His Church to be participants with Him in reigning over the nations of the world.

God Reigning in His World

That God reigns in individual lives is accepted in all of the Christian community. That God reigns as the King of the Church is accepted in most of the Christian community, but, unfortunately, this is where the reign of God stops in the minds of most people, believers and unbelievers alike. However, David did not see God as King merely over Israel (a type of the Church); he spoke of God as being the highest Potentate over every king or kingdom on the face of this earth. "Because of thy temple at Jerusalem," he wrote, "shall kings bring presents unto thee" (Psalms 68:29). Somehow David felt that God was King of kings in the here and now, not merely in the hereafter, for when the Ark of God was placed in the tent that David had pitched for it, he had the choir sing, "Let the heavens be glad, and let the earth rejoice: and let men say among the nations, *The Lord reigneth*" (1 Chronicles 16:31, italics added).

This theme that the Lord reigneth (always in the present progressive tense) is heralded loudly throughout the Scriptures. In the Pentateuch, Moses sings, "The Lord shall reign for ever and ever" (Exodus 15:18). In the historic books it was David's choral number that proclaimed, "The Lord reigneth" (1 Chronicles 16:31), while in the poetic books it is the Psalter that repeats, "The Lord reigneth" (Psalms 93:1; 97:1; 99:1). Among the major prophets, Isaiah cries, "Thy God reigneth!" (Isaiah 52:7), while Micah speaks for the minor prophets in declaring, ". . . The Lord shall reign over them in mount Zion from henceforth, even for ever" (Micah 4:7). Furthermore, I have already projected, the New Testament abounds with the theology of God, through Christ, reigning in life, in the Church, and in the world, and it ends by declaring, "Alleluia: for the Lord God omnipotent reigneth" (Revelation 19:6). So the Word consistently teaches that God is now King over all the earth, whether or not it appears that way to the natural man.

The rather popular philosophy that satan is the god of this world, but that someday Jehovah God will overthrow him and become the ruler of this world, is overly simplistic and not soundly rooted in the Scriptures. It makes the devil too large and God too small and almost equates the power of evil with the power of God's goodness. While I recognize that Paul's statement "In whom the god of this world hath blinded the minds of them which believe not . . ." (2 Corinthians 4:4) is generally considered to refer to satan, I would hasten to point out that the very same word is used in Paul's statement about ' . . . the enemies of the cross of Christ: Whose end is destruction, whose God is their belly . . ." (Philippians 3:18,19). In both cases Paul uses the word *theos* as the Greeks used it in their polytheistic society, not as the Bible uses it in its monotheistic philosophy. From this one single statement we have no more right to make satan the god of this world than we have to make man's belly the god of this world. There has never been any other God over this world than the Almighty God who has revealed Himself as Father, Son, and Holy Spirit.

Both the Old and the New Testaments declare, "The earth is the Lord's, and the fulness thereof" (Psalms 24:1; 1 Corinthians 10:26,28). This psalm adds, "and they that dwell therein. For he hath founded it upon the seas, and established it upon the floods" (Psalms 24:1,2). This world is God's by right of creation; it is the work of His hands. He never gave possession of it to Adam; Adam was merely the gardener in Eden. Although through sin Adam seems to have relinquished his rights and authorities, satan did not gain possession of the world, for Adam did not have possession of this world. The only dominion God had granted to Adam was "over the fish of the sea, and over fowl of the air, and over every living thing that moveth upon the earth" (Genesis 1:28). These satan may have wrested from the control of Adam, but this hardly gives him title deed to the earth and its fullness, to say nothing of dominion over men.

Satan only wrested authority from man; he did not force God to relinquish control of anything. Satan has never successfully taken anything out of the hand of God, and he never will, as Jesus so firmly stated in His high priestly prayer (*see* John 17:12).

This is not the devil's world; this is my Father's world! "For the kingdom is the Lord's; and he is the governor among the nations" (Psalms 22:28), the psalmist declares. He has neither abandoned this world nor surrendered it to satan. Instead, at a price beyond our comprehension, He has redeemed both men and the earth itself from the curse of the fall, and He has pledged that the consummation of that redemption will follow the second coming of Christ.

"If satan is not the god of this world," you may ask, "what is his role here on the earth?" Jesus repeatedly called him the "prince of the world" (John 12:31; 14:30; 16:11), and Paul called him "the prince of the power of the air" (Ephesians 2:2). The Greek word both of them use is *archon*, which means "chief," "to rule," or "a leader." That satan is a leader and a ruler is indisputable, but that hardly makes a god out of him. This same Greek word is used of Christ, of rulers of nations, of judges and magistrates, and of members of the Sanhedrin as well as of satan. In the Old Testament God's mighty angel is called "prince" (*see* Daniel 10:21; 12:1).

In God's heaven, Lucifer was "the anointed cherub that covereth" (Ezekiel 28:14). Through his lusting to be ". . . like the most High" (Isaiah 14:14) ". . . he was cast out into the earth; and his angels were cast out with him" (Revelation 12:9). Being deposed from heaven did not elevate him to the status of a god; instead, it took his very name "Lucifer" from him, leaving him with titles such as "devil," "satan," "serpent," "dragon," and "deceiver" (*see* Revelation 12:9). He was a prince, and he remains a prince. He was under God's orders, and he remains under God's orders. He had to obey the Word of God implicitly, and he remains subject to the commands of God to this very day. If satan took Adam's position of gardener away from him, then it is now up to satan to pull the weeds out of God's garden, but being the gardener does not give title to the garden to him any more than it would to a horticulturist today, for tilling the land does not give title to that land. God owns this earth, even if satan tills part of it.

Admittedly, the issue in most people's minds is not so much the ownership of this world as the government of the world. "Who reigns over the earth now?" is the immediate question. As sovereign God and as King of all kings, God has the ultimate rulership over all things. He rules and overrules in all the affairs of this earth. Nonetheless, through Adam's fall, satan, as the prince of the world, found himself in a strong governmental position in the affairs of men. He influences the attitudes and actions of great hosts of men, and he has special princes from among the angels that fell with him who have been given authority over nations of this world. Although they are mighty, they are not even so mighty as God's angels, so far are they beneath God Himself.

That God is allowing wickedness a period of time in which to mature seems to be clearly taught in the Scriptures. Even satan is allowed to do his utmost to harness the rebellion of wicked men to wage a frontal attack on God in a final attempt to dethrone Him, but "God has allowed us to know the secret of his plan, and it is this: he purposes in His sovereign will that all human history shall be consummated in Christ, that everything that exists in Heaven or earth shall find its perfection and fulfilment in him" (Ephesians 1:9,10 PHILLIPS).

God is so completely in control of this world that He dares to allow satan to function in his rebellion, within predetermined limits, knowing that at any moment the divine will can be enforced upon the entire world, for, after all, satan must work through men, and God Himself controls the life and death of men. When the works of satan go beyond what is best for God's Church on earth, God need do little more than withdraw the breath of life from a few key men, and the entire scheme is frustrated. Satan works long and hard, but God controls the results of that labor. Satan put Peter in jail, but God's angel released him. Satan put Paul in jail, but God made a writer of the New Testament out of him while he was in seclusion. Satan mercilessly persecuted the early Church, but God caused the blood of martyrs to become the seed of the Church. Satan can never do anything that God cannot undo, overdo, and outdo within an instant of time.

David seemed to intuitively know this, or else divine revelation had come to him, for all of his psalms carry this theme of the sovereignty of God. He never visualizes God on the defensive or in defeat, for he sees God reigning in all situations of life. He consistently sees God as ". . . the King of all the earth." ". . . God reigneth over the heathen," he cried, "God sitteth upon the throne of his holiness" (Psalms 47:7,8).

David was so assured of God's rulership over the entire world that when the Ark was secure in the little tent he had prepared for it in Jerusalem, he declared, "Because of thy temple at Jerusalem shall kings bring presents unto thee" (Psalms 68:29). It is rather interesting that it is not because of God's throne but because of God's Temple that kings would come to Him. It is the priestly ministry of Christ that draws men voluntarily to Him. He is the Priest-King, and He will indeed rule in Jerusalem as King, but David says that submission to Him on a voluntary basis will be because the Temple is there and they are responding to God in worship.

But, of course, not all will worship God voluntarily, so David speaks of God bringing the rebels into submission by force. "Rebuke our enemies, O Lord. Bring them – submissive, tax in hand . . ." (Psalms 68:30 TLB). There will be a day when nations will be forced to come under God's law and to submit to His government. All rebellion will meet rebuke, and redemption for them will require the bringing of an assessment to God.

Furthermore, David calls upon God to "scatter all who delight in war" (Psalms 68:30 TLB). From the tower of Babel right on to the end of time, God scattered the enemies He chose not to destroy, for scattering happens to be one of God's favorite weapons against men. If there is any hope of bringing His enemies back into submission, God merely scatters them so that their united effort is broken until in their frustration they call upon God. David saw a day in which men who hate would not be able to bring their hatred into a coalition force before God scattered them. The Prince of Peace will yet reign over men!

David enthusiastically adds, "Princes shall come out of Egypt; Ethiopia shall soon stretch out her hands unto God" (Psalms 68:31), as he gathers prophetic insight concerning the last days. Eschatologically, most Christians believe in the coming rule and reign of Jesus Christ on this earth. We still expect him to set up an earthly kingdom with Jerusalem as His headquarters, and to rule the nations with a rod of iron. We expect the saints to rule and reign with Christ in that day of righteousness and peace, and in that day all nations will come to worship God in Jerusalem, or there will be no rain upon their lands (*see* Zechariah 14:17).

"Be still, and know that I am God: I will be exalted among the heathen, I will be exalted in the earth" (Psalms 46:10), David wrote. Even more excitedly he proclaimed, ". . . through the greatness of thy power shall thine enemies submit themselves unto thee. All the earth shall worship thee, and shall sing unto thee; they shall sing to thy name (Psalms 66:3,4), and as a warning to the rebellious he wrote, "He ruleth by his power for ever; his eyes behold the nations: let not the rebellious exalt themselves. Selah" (Psalms 66:7).

There is so much we do not know about the future, but of one thing we are certain: God who rules shall extend that rule to include every king and ruler, every nation, and every person. He will be King forever, and we have been invited to sit together with Him on His throne and to share His authority and reign.

From the cry of God which pierced down into the depths of hell when His Son lay in the grave, to the shout and the trump of God (*see* 1 Thessalonians 4:16) when His Son returns to the earth, the call "Let God arise" has been and always will be the shout of triumph which nothing can successfully withstand.

"God shall arise . . ." (Berkeley).

"God is already beginning to arise . . ." (AMPLIFIED).

"LET GOD ARISE . . ." (Psalms 68:1).

Whose faith is it anyway?
Michael S.B. Reid

With the advent of such strong emphasis put on faith today we must ask ourselves the questions....

Why have prayers gone unanswered?

Why are there so many sick?

Why are so many churches filled with the lame, halt, deaf and blind, both physically and spiritually?

Why have so many heard sermons on divine healing and salvation that are true to the Scriptures – and yet are not healed or brought to life?

Within this book are some answers to these very questions.

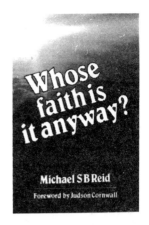

Let God Arise!
Judson Cornwall

Now, as seldom before, there is an inner awareness that God is about to do a fresh new thing in the world. The prophets are declaring that a new visitation of God is imminent. God is declaring that this visitation will begin in the United States, New Zealand and England, and that this three-pronged offensive will encompass the world in a rapid move of God's Spirit that will reveal God the Father in such a way as to induce holiness and produce worship. Already there are scattered groups of Christians in these countries that seem to be forerunners of this visitation.

Secrets of the Kingdom
Dr. R. Edward Miller

God speaks to man through types, symbols and parables.

...Hidden within this book are the secret treasures of God's Kingdom.

Dr. Miller has shown insights that have been birthed in his heart during revival fires. Today few men can reveal so vividly the principles of the Kingdom and Ways of God.

David worshiped a living God
Judson Cornwall

This is Judson's newest book on praise and worship,
destined to be a classic as it describes in beautiful
detail the names of God and what they mean to the
worshiping saint.

The Rebirth of Music
LaMar Boschman

What is the real purpose of music in the church? Is it
merely to entertain? Is it just for evangelistic purposes?
In this revolutionary book, you will discover the unique
position that music has in God's plan for His people.
You will learn what the Bible teaches about music's
function in praise and worship, as well as how you can
be a part of the restoration of music to its rightful
place in the Church.

Exploring Worship
Bob Sorge

A practical guide to praise and worship. This book fills
the need for instruction for people whose hearts are
ablaze to worship God in a deeper way and for people
whose desire is to lead others into that same place. It
gives practical answers about entering the presence of
God, moving prophetically in praise and worship, and
planning a worship service. Nothing else like it on the
market!

Titles available from your local Christian Bookseller
or direct from Sharon Publications Ltd.

Leaders - Eat What You Serve
Dr. Judson Cornwall - £4.95

Burned out - Dropped out - Forced out
These dreadful terms have become too commonly
used when describing those who carry the mantle of
servanthood in the church. Yet there are ways of
dealing with these situations that are most often found
in our own sermon notebooks. Leaders must learn to
EAT WHAT YOU SERVE. The same relationship
with Jesus that we encourage others with is the same
relationship that changes and strengthens the leader's
life as well.

Leaders need Him just as their flocks do!

"We need an infusion of Christ's life more than we
need a vacation from His work"

Cry for me Argentina -
Dr. Edward Miller - £2.95

Here is the factual background to one of the greatest
spiritual awakenings in the history of the Christian
Church ... and it happened in our day.

In this personal, first-hand account we are taken
behind the scenes to discover the why? ... and how?
To anyone earnestly in pursuit of God, his ways and
principles of operation, this vivid account will disclose
many of God's secrets.

The message contained herein will challenge and
deeply inspire. Upon a prepared few will settle the
conviction that "our God is the same yesterday, today,
and forever and is without respect of person. We can
find God's way through to a glorious revival for
ourselves, our church, our town, our area, yes, and
even our country!"

Revival begins in City Bell
Dr. R. Edward Miller

Heaven
Judson Cornwall

In his best writing tradition, Judson has given us
another classic. Here is a book for those who love
heaven! Learn where it's located; why we hope for it;
who lives there; why it's so wonderful; how to begin to
live in heaven, here on earth.

Victory in Adversity -
Dr. Edward Miller - £2.95

This book shows the victory God wrought in various Bible
characters through tremendously adverse circumstances,
and how they triumphed in them.

I looked and I saw the Lord -
Annie - £2.95

This book is by Dr. Miller's adopted daughter Annie who
was wonderfully converted during the revival in Argentina.
God opened her eyes to see into the heavenlies. The
experiences recorded and visions conveyed are a privilege
to read and share.

I looked and I saw Mysteries -
Annie - £2.95

Annie's encounter with God burned into her heart a deep,
constant desire to seek Jesus and to "pray through" until
she entered His presence every day. As she faithfully
sought Him, He taught her things in accordance with the
Scriptures that she could not have known before.
Afterwards, she would share what she had seen and she had
the visions explained to her. Not knowing the Bible, she
hadn't a clue as to the visions' meaning.